Linguistics

Linguistics
FOR STUDENTS
OF
New
Testament
Greek

A Survey of Basic Concepts
and Applications

David Alan Black

Foreword by
Moisés Silva

BAKER BOOK HOUSE
Grand Rapids, Michigan 49516

Library of Congress Cataloging-in-Publication Data

Black, David Alan, 1952-
 Linguistics for students of New Testament Greek.

 Some text in New Testament Greek.
 Includes bibliographies and index.
 1. Greek language, Biblical—Grammar.   2. Bible
N.T.—Language, style.   I. Title.
PA817.B55   1988   487'.4   88-3494
ISBN 0-8010-0949-9

To **Dr. Richard Mayhue,**
senior pastor of the historic Grace Brethren Church of Long
Beach, whose commitment to biblical Christianity and steady
enthusiasm for my work I have constantly valued.

Contents

Foreword

A quarter of a century ago, James Barr's publications were unique in calling biblical scholars to become familiar with the field of general linguistics and to integrate its results with the work of exegesis. In spite of many favorable reviews of his books, the scholarly response to Barr was mixed, and even those who agreed with him usually did little more than pay lip service to the value of linguistics. Even during the 1970s, significant works in this area were few and far between.

The 1980s, however, have seen a genuine awakening to the substantive contribution that linguistics can make to biblical exegesis. Valuable books in this field are no longer rare, while articles and monographs regularly present the more technical aspects of this interdisciplinary approach.

Yet one must not conclude that these developments, important though they are, have had a major impact on biblical studies. The vast majority of publications in the areas of exegesis and biblical theology reflect only a superficial acquaintance (if any) with modern linguistics. While biblical commentators, for example, are expected to make responsible use of ancillary disciplines—such as archaeology, textual criticism, classical studies, and so on— linguistic theory is virtually absent from the standard commentaries, even though a commentator must deal constantly with the nature of language before drawing exegetical conclusions.

The fault, to be sure, does not lie primarily in the field of biblical scholarship, since general linguistics has not yet been fully integrated into the liberal arts curriculum. Theological seminaries can still expect new students to have taken courses in history, literature, philosophy, and the sciences, but only a small percentage of college graduates have had formal exposure to linguistics (though happily an increasing number of English programs now incorporate the principles and methods of this discipline in their required courses). Since a seminary can hardly justify offering required courses in linguistics, some ingenuity is necessary if the theological curriculum is to remedy this particular deficiency.

This is precisely where Dr. Black's book offers an important contribution. The reader will not find in these pages a mere introduction to linguistics with scattered biblical examples; nor is this work a Greek grammar with occasional forays into linguistics. Instead, and perceptively, the author has chosen to instruct the reader simultaneously in both fields. The value of this approach is indisputable. Most students have neither the interest nor the time to read extensively in linguistics per se and then to integrate what they have read into their study of the biblical languages. The present work blends the two steps into one—and it does so without creating confusion. In fact, most theological students, after going through this book, will have a much better grasp of *both* linguistics and Greek grammar than if they had read two separate textbooks.

Accordingly, this work is ideally suited for reviewing Greek grammar. Not only intermediate students of the language, but also pastors and even scholars who have allowed their Greek to become a little rusty, can profit greatly from a careful study of the material presented here. They will certainly learn many new things. Perhaps more important, however, is the new perspective they will acquire on things they already know ("So that's what that strange rule was all about!").

Dr. Black does not, of course, intend to replace the standard intermediate Greek grammars. Indeed, some users may wish that he had placed greater emphasis on matters of syntax (I myself might handle the problem of verbal aspect a little differently). But the book has a clearly defined purpose, and the author has been very successful in reaching his specific goal. The publication of this book, I am convinced, will enrich the theological curriculum and have a notable impact on the next generation of biblical exegetes.

Moisés Silva
Westminster Theological Seminary

Preface

Not long ago, Greek students lived in a stable, protected world where the rules were known, where there were established methods, and where traditional grammars made up the bulk of teaching materials. Today, this closed and protected world is opening up and branching out, rediscovering the outside world. No Greek student is an island: like it or not, he is asked to ponder the relationship between Greek and the science of linguistics. Both the content and the spirit of traditional instruction in grammar are being challenged in fundamental ways by the revolution in language scholarship brought about by modern linguistic research. Linguistics has brought with it new terms and new procedures but above all a new attitude. The language teacher once treated grammar as if it were something known and absolute. There was no need to ask: Where should we start if we wish to develop a system of grammar? What is the best method of teaching grammar? What in fact *is* grammar? Linguists set out to convince language teachers of the need for starting from the foundations.

As a consequence, interest in linguistics among teachers and students of New Testament Greek has risen phenomenally in the last few years. The subject is in the air at every professional meeting—sometimes earnestly advocated, sometimes bitterly condemned, but never completely ignored. This curiosity about linguistics and its place in the study of Greek is now too great to be satisfied by the handful of specialized studies written mostly for experts. Clearly there is a need for books that will introduce

Greek students to the field of linguistics and show how its findings can increase their understanding of the New Testament.

This book is one Greek teacher's contribution toward meeting this need. It is primarily concerned, as its title suggests, with the interrelations between linguistics and New Testament Greek grammar. It is not a textbook on either subject, and should not be expected to give an advanced view of either (as its subtitle conveys). Instead, the book grew out of a practical need to give a basic course in linguistics for New Testament students. I hope that it will also be of service to many other teachers giving similar courses in universities and seminaries. Those who are studying Greek in the usual way should find the book helpful in the application of linguistics to their knowledge of the language. Others can use the book in private study as the means of acquiring in the shortest and most direct way a sufficient knowledge of linguistics to enable them to move on to more advanced works. I even cherish the dream that teachers will learn something valuable about the nature of Greek from this text and that this knowledge will improve their teaching and help their students.

A word on how this book is to be used. It is an introduction and a survey, to be read rather than consulted. The material is presented sequentially: the student is first introduced to the phenomenon of language study itself, and then to an integrated description of New Testament Greek, using whichever linguistic theory that applies most directly to the descriptive problem at hand. I have done my best to eliminate unnecessary terminology and to define new terms. I have also decided against using footnotes since the book will be easier to read without endless qualifications and references. Most of the concepts presented here are not original, but are drawn eclectically from a wide range of authors within the general field of linguistics. At the end of each chapter there is a short bibliography listing important books and articles that have been consulted and that any student who has mastered this book might wish to read in the future.

It is superfluous to point out that a book of this size does not exhaust its subject. This was not my aim, as it is far beyond my gifts. I have merely tried to present, as simply as possible, the generally accepted facts and principles of linguistics as they apply to New Testament Greek. Linguistics is like the proverbial hydra— a monster with an endless number of heads. There seems to be no limit to the aspects of this subject that one could explore.

rightened the task of teaching Greek grammar and
eir stimulating questions, observations, and challenges
nal wisdom have illuminated many a classroom dis-
well as my own academic life, and it is to them and
ors that this book is affectionately directed.

Consequently I have felt it necessary to specialize quite rigidly, and in the process much had to be diluted, omitted, or condensed. Thus in many areas the presentation will be sketchy, though, I hope, accurate. If at times the language in this book seems too nontechnical, too simple to express significant and complex concepts, I would ask the reader to keep in mind that the anticipated user of this book is not the professional linguist, comfortably conversant with Chomsky, Pike, and others, but the busy student pursuing a working knowledge of Greek. And to the degree that I have whetted the student's appetite to delve deeper into the Greek language—far beyond the scope of this book—I can say that I have achieved my goal in writing.

years have
exegesis. T
to conventi
cussion as
their succes

Acknowledgme

It is a pleasure to render
significantly contributed to
teachers at Basel, notably th
work exemplified the essentia
and biblical scholarship, and
never be forgotten. More
support: Dr. Harwood Hess
guistics, who read the manu
comments helped me to for
ideas; Mr. Richard Hoffman
concern and counsel were a
and Mr. Larry Marshburn o
kind arrangements for loani
the research and writing.

I cannot sufficiently expres
Baker Book House for his en
to Ms. Maria Bulgarello, assis
during the final stages of the
Miss Janet LaBarge and Mrs
typing, and to Mr. Richard
special measure of apprecia
Westminster Theological Se
write the foreword and who
constructive criticism.

I owe a sincere "thank yo
Nathan and Matthew, who
patience, and forgiveness are
Finally, I am grateful to those

1

Introducing Linguistics: The Landscape and the Quest

Why Study Linguistics?

This book is an invitation to think about language. It attempts to apply the principles of linguistic science to the analysis of New Testament Greek. It is intended for use by those without any prior knowledge of linguistics who desire a straightforward, practical, and relaxed introduction to the subject.

Unfortunately, many students (particularly those who were frightened by grammar early in life and have never fully recovered) fail to learn linguistics simply because they are scared off by the word itself. The grammar-shy student takes one look at it and falls into a faint, certain that he has met the evil eye itself.

Actually, linguistics is no more formidable than any other course of study. Our anxiety stems from certain mistaken ideas about linguistics. Some of these notions are minor, like loose buttons or untied shoelaces; others are as threatening as the San Andreas Fault. But the Terrible Three are the following:

The terms used in linguistics are too difficult for me to understand. This objection is perfectly reasonable, especially to busy students who have little use for "phonemes" or "morphemes" if such terms seem to be unnecessary verbiage. But the language of linguistics is no more strange or esoteric than much of the vocabulary we use every day. Every field, every profession has its jargon—special words to describe what it does and how it does it. Dentists talk about "caries" instead of cavities. Teachers talk about "learning objectives" when they refer to what they are trying to accomplish. A student's vocabulary may range all the way from dispensing "superunleaded" or eating "BLTs" to debating "the eschatology of the Olivet Discourse"—all in the same day! Mastering the terminology of linguistics is simply a matter of learning what various words mean and how they are used.

I could never hope to master all of the topics covered in linguistics. There is, of course, nothing unusual about this apprehension. Most modern sciences are fairly well developed and perpetuated by specialists in the field. But every expert began as a newcomer in his area of specialization, not as an accomplished scholar. The complexity of linguistics, therefore, is in no way unique, and beginners should no more be deterred from studying it because of the enormity of the field than beginners in astronomy should become discouraged by the impossibility of learning the name of every star in the heavens.

Linguists themselves seem uncertain about their conclusions, and the entire discipline is in a state of flux. Why, then, should I enter this "jungle"? Controversies and rapid shifts in the linguistic camp clearly exist. But they should not prevent us from asking the basic questions: What have we learned from linguistics over the years? What are the lasting contributions that linguists have made to the way we understand language? What aspects of the linguists' work have proved most stimulating and productive in the classroom? In challenging much in our methodology and teaching that was negative or merely conventional, linguists have opened up an exciting world of new materials and ideas for us to draw on.

These three misconceptions about linguistics are not the only ones, but they are the most common—and the most likely to cause offense to the beginning student. Each has a superficial attractiveness, starting from facts that are well known but drawing exaggerated and unjustified conclusions from them. The easiest way to handle the Terrible Three is to forget about them. Put them behind you forever. Then you can devote your energies to learning and applying linguistics in your study of New Testament Greek. It may be a slow, laborious process at first, but gradually you will find that comprehension comes easily; you will have fewer and fewer apprehensions about linguistics because your heightened awareness of possible misconceptions will help you avoid them from the start. Today there is a plethora of fresh, substantial, challenging materials that can help teachers and students understand and use the Greek language.

Consequently I have felt it necessary to specialize quite rigidly, and in the process much had to be diluted, omitted, or condensed. Thus in many areas the presentation will be sketchy, though, I hope, accurate. If at times the language in this book seems too nontechnical, too simple to express significant and complex concepts, I would ask the reader to keep in mind that the anticipated user of this book is not the professional linguist, comfortably conversant with Chomsky, Pike, and others, but the busy student pursuing a working knowledge of Greek. And to the degree that I have whetted the student's appetite to delve deeper into the Greek language—far beyond the scope of this book—I can say that I have achieved my goal in writing.

Acknowledgments

It is a pleasure to render thanks to many people who have significantly contributed to this work, stretching back to my teachers at Basel, notably the late Dr. Bo Reicke, whose lifetime work exemplified the essential relationship between the humanities and biblical scholarship, and whose charity and friendship will never be forgotten. More recently, several friends have given support: Dr. Harwood Hess of the Summer Institute of Linguistics, who read the manuscript in its early stages and whose comments helped me to formulate and clarify my material and ideas; Mr. Richard Hoffman of Wycliffe Bible Translators, whose concern and counsel were a continual source of encouragement; and Mr. Larry Marshburn of the Biola University library, whose kind arrangements for loaning out books considerably facilitated the research and writing.

I cannot sufficiently express my thanks to Mr. Allan Fisher of Baker Book House for his enthusiastic support of this project, and to Ms. Maria Bulgarello, assistant editor, for her advice and work during the final stages of the editing. I must also extend thanks to Miss Janet LaBarge and Mrs. Kathy Lemp for their assistance in typing, and to Mr. Richard Zuelch for preparing the indexes. A special measure of appreciation goes to Dr. Moisés Silva of Westminster Theological Seminary, who graciously consented to write the foreword and who was also kind enough to offer some constructive criticism.

I owe a sincere "thank you" to my wife Becky and my sons Nathan and Matthew, whose love, support, encouragement, patience, and forgiveness are an indispensable part of my work. Finally, I am grateful to those excellent students who for a dozen years have brightened the task of teaching Greek grammar and exegesis. Their stimulating questions, observations, and challenges to conventional wisdom have illuminated many a classroom discussion as well as my own academic life, and it is to them and their successors that this book is affectionately directed.

To use such materials productively, however, linguists must be prepared to answer the questions any bright student might legitimately ask:

What are we after? What we are after in studying linguistics is not to commit ourselves to memorizing a new system of rules or a new set of terms. What we are after is to develop a fuller awareness and appreciation of the nature of language itself. By studying linguistics we gain insight into what language is and how it works. We acquire basic knowledge about the analysis and description of languages on this earth, and about ways in which human beings use language to communicate with one another. Knowledge of Greek words and forms is of little help without this understanding of the essential character of language.

What is it good for? When we study linguistics we are learning how to put the Greek language in its rightful place as a part—perhaps the most technical part—of our work in the text of the New Testament. Through exposure and practice, we can acquire a broader, more confident command of New Testament Greek. We can learn why the future of ἔχω has the rough breathing—an apparent "exception"; why the reduplication of τίθημι "breaks the rules" (it should be θίθημι); how the so-called irregular verbs such as βαίνω are based on consistent linguistic principles; why ἔργον and *work* are only superficially different in form.

But more importantly, the study of linguistics can contribute a great deal to our understanding of the *meaning* of the New Testament. It can help us become more aware of why we understand a text the way we do when we read it, and it can help us talk about the text more precisely, by providing us with a methodology through which we can show how interpretation is in part derived from grammatical considerations. Linguistics may also help solve problems of interpretation by showing us why one meaning is possible but not another. Above all, however, linguistics can give us a point of view, a way of looking at a text that will help us develop a consistent analysis, and prompt us to ask questions about the language of the text that we might have otherwise overlooked.

How, then, does one study linguistics properly? You must begin by finding out exactly what it is and how it is put together. Then you can learn how to organize your own thoughts scientifically and objectively. With each chapter of this book you will delve deeper and deeper into the Greek language, studying progressively its various features, evaluating the subject matter as you go, and making new discoveries about language in the process. By the time you have finished this book, you should have learned enough about linguistics to significantly improve your language skills.

This chapter introduces most of the major questions a linguist would ask when investigating the structure and use of Greek, and shows how the linguist's observations can be brought to bear on the study of the New Testament and its interpretation. We cannot satisfactorily proceed, however, without defining two of the most basic terms: *linguist* and *linguistics*.

What Is a Linguist?

A person who studies human language is usually referred to as a *linguist*. *Linguistician*, a term coined by Robert Hall on the analogy of *mathematician* or *mortician*, more accurately describes one who works scientifically in language, but it is too much of a tongue twister to become generally accepted. Sometimes the word *linguist* is also used to refer to a "polyglot," that is, a person who can speak or write several languages (Gk. πολύς, 'many' + γλῶσσα, 'language').* The scientific linguist, however, is not particularly interested in actually using language for communication. He may, in fact, speak only his native tongue. A linguist in the sense of a linguistics expert can be likened to a musicologist. A musicologist could analyze a piano concerto by pointing out its themes, movements, meter, and tempo. But he need not be able to play the concerto himself. He leaves that to the concert pianist. Likewise it is more important for the linguist to analyze and explain linguistic phenomena such as German verbs and French nouns than to make himself understood in Berlin or Paris.

The linguist's work is understanding and describing the nature of language. He tries to answer such basic questions as "What is language?" and "How does language work?" He probes into various related problems, such as "Why do languages change?", "What do all languages have in common?", "How does a child learn to speak?", and so on. Linguists, of course, are not the only scholars concerned with these questions. In studying language scientifically, anthropologists, psychologists, sociologists, missiologists, biblical scholars, and many others gain important insights into their own areas of specialization. But before such scholars can

---

* The etymologies given in this text are for illustrative purposes and are not necessarily guides to meaning.

develop adequate theories of language relating to their own disciplines, they must first understand the essential nature of language. Linguistics provides this understanding and thus serves as a bridge between language proper and related fields.

What Is Linguistics?

Linguistics is the science that attempts to understand language from the point of view of its "inner workings"—what linguists call *internal structure*. This structure includes speech sounds and meanings, as well as a complex grammatical system that relates those sounds and meanings. The analysis of a language system is possible only by examining and comparing actual manifestations of language as represented by samples of speech or writing, but the end result is a description of the "linguistic code" that more or less uniformly manifests itself in all verbal communication. Notice that this definition of linguistics maintains a distinction between the language system (*la langue*) and the manifestation of that system in the speech of particular individuals (*la parole*). This distinction was emphasized by the Swiss linguist Ferdinand de Saussure, who pointed out that linguistics is concerned with the study of *la langue*, the language system.

In brief, then, linguistics may be defined as the scientific study of the language systems of the world. It is a science because the empirical methods of the sciences are used as much as possible to bring the precision and control of scientific investigation to the study of language. Linguistics is not, of course, wholly autonomous. It must draw upon such sciences as physiology, psychology, anthropology, and sociology for certain basic concepts and data. But however closely it may be related to other sciences, linguistics is unique insofar as it is interested in language as an end in itself.

How Do Linguists Go About Their Work?

Because language is one of the most complex of human activities, linguistics has developed into a full-blown academic field with many specialized yet interdependent disciplines that concentrate on specific aspects of language. Linguists can take certain general approaches to the study of language. First, there is the synchronic approach (Gk. σύν, 'with' + χρόνος, 'time'), in which language is viewed as it exists at some particular point in time. *Descriptive linguistics* is essentially a synchronic view of language, examining language without reference to the changes that are a natural part of the development of any language. Second, linguists can take a diachronic approach (Gk. διά, 'through' + χρόνος, 'time'), viewing language from a historical perspective. Included in this area is *historical linguistics*, the study of the origin and development of the sound patterns of language, of the forms of individual words, of the grammatical relationships between words, and of all other data related to language. A third approach to language study, the *comparative* (Lat. *comparo*, 'I couple, compare'), investigates the possible relationships between individual languages as well as variations within the same language (dialects).

Let us now take a closer look at these approaches to the study of language. We shall describe each one briefly in this chapter, and then in succeeding chapters investigate them more thoroughly.

Descriptive Linguistics

The grammar of a language is the chief concern of the descriptive linguist. *Grammar* can be defined as a system of rules relating sound and meaning. The attempt to identify and classify all the sounds used in a given language is known as *phonology* (Gk. φωνή, 'sound' + λόγος, 'word, science'). Phonologists listen to speech and try to break it down into its constituent parts. Among the basic phonological units of all human sound systems are discrete elements called *phonemes*—the smallest units of sound that make a functional difference in the meaning of words. The method used to determine the phonemes of a language is to contrast words that are identical in every sound except one, and then determine if the meanings of the two words are the same or different. For example, the words *pill* and *bill* are identical in every respect except the initial sound. It would seem that *p* and *b* are separate phonemes in English. This conclusion is confirmed by noting the difference in meaning between *rapid* and *rabid*. English has approximately forty-five such phonemes.

The next layer of the structure of language is its *morphology* (Gk. μορφή, 'form'). Morphologists are interested in the particles of meaning, known as *morphemes*, that are put together to form words. A morpheme is distinguished from a phoneme by the fact that a morpheme, by itself, has meaning, whereas a phoneme, by itself, does not. For instance, the phoneme *b* carries with it no particular meaning, but when combined with the phoneme *e*, the sound that results (*be*) does have meaning. The word *be* is thus identifiable as an English morpheme.

Morphologists classify words into at least two categories: *simple* and *complex*. A simple word such as *dog* seems to be an irreducible unit: there seems to be no way to break it down further into meaningful parts. On the other hand, the word *dogs* seems to be made up of two parts: the noun *dog* and a plural ending (*-s* in this case). Not every noun in English forms its plural in this fashion, but many do. In linguistics these meaning-bearing parts of a complex word—that is, the different building blocks that make it up—are also identified as morphemes. In this case we say that we have the plural morpheme *-s*; and in addition, we say that the simple noun *dog* is itself a morpheme. Morphemes, then, are often defined as the minimal units of meaning in a language: they can be broken down no further into meaningful parts.

The closest thing to morphology in traditional grammar is the "prefixes-suffixes-and-roots" approach to word analysis. Linguists, however, have refined word analysis to the point of reconstructing the complex morphological structure of a language and comparing this structure with similar structures in other languages. Some morphologists have even classified languages according to the way in which morphemes are put together to form words. *Agglutinative* languages (Lat. *ad*, 'to' + *glutino*, 'I glue') are those that tend to combine long strings of morphemes into a single word. An interesting example comes from Swahili, in which a word that sounds something like *atanipenda* means "he will like me," but a change to *atakupenda* makes it "he will like you." *Polysynthetic* languages (Gk. πολύς, 'many' + σύνθεσις, 'combination') are even more agglutinative in their formation of words. The classic example is a polysynthetic Eskimo word that means "I am looking for something suitable for a fish line." On the other hand, *isolating* languages, such as English, have a tendency to use shorter words. In the above example, a speaker of English must use several independent words to say what a speaker of the Eskimo language might say in a single word. Isolating languages depend more on word order than on word combinations to achieve meaning. Finally, *inflectional* languages, such as Latin, have an elaborate system of word endings for nouns, verbs, and other parts of speech. These endings indicate such things as tense, number, gender, and case.

Greek is one language that indicates practically everything by inflection. The Greek equivalent for "I shall hear" is ἀκούσω, where the basic meaning "hear" is conveyed by ἀκου, the idea that the action will take place in the future is indicated by σ, and the fact that "I" will perform the action (first person singular) is shown by the ω at the end of the word. English, instead, uses three separate words arranged in a certain order: a subject pronoun *I*, a helping verb (auxiliary) *shall*, which by itself would not mean much, and the basic verb *hear*. German handles this situation as English does (*ich werde hören*), Spanish as Greek (*oiré*), while French has an interesting combination of both (*j'entendrai*); here French indicates the subject "I" twice, by the ending *-ai*, and also by the subject pronoun *j'* (for *je*)—much like a man who wears both suspenders and a belt!

Morphologists, then, take a close look at a word to see how it is made, examining it apart from a sentence just as we might examine a carburetor apart from an engine or a single musical bar apart from a whole composition. A word has a certain wholeness and independence of its own; it can stand alone and still make some sense. However, no matter how well a word stands alone it is usually just one small part of a larger whole—the sentence itself. And in order to do its part in the whole operation, it must connect smoothly with the parts around it.

To put this another way, a group of words written down at random can be likened to the pieces of a jigsaw puzzle laying on a table—we see a confusing collection of shapes and colors, with only the vaguest hint of a pattern:

language, men, the, foreign, a, learned

It is only when we place each piece in its correct position that a meaningful picture emerges:

The men learned a foreign language.

Words will remain in such a meaningless condition until we provide them with some kind of structural sense, or structural meaning. The term *structural meaning* refers to such ideas as subject, object, tense, number, and so on. Thus, in the sentence "The men learned a foreign language" we are told who did the learning (subject), what was learned (object), and something about the time of the event (tense). Notice that this was largely accomplished by arranging the words in a particular order (subject, verb, object). In Greek, however, the order of words is not nearly as important as in English. The sentence "The men learned a foreign language" could be expressed in Greek not only by ξένην γλῶσσαν ἔμαθον οἱ ἄνδρες, but also by ἔμαθον οἱ ἄνδρες ξένην γλῶσσαν, οἱ ἄνδρες γλῶσσαν ξένην ἔμαθον, γλῶσσαν ἔμαθον οἱ ἄνδρες ξένην, and some twenty-two other possibilities!

Every language in the world has a system for putting words together. The way in which speakers of a language pattern words is generally referred to as the *syntax* of that language (Gk. σύνταξις, 'a putting together'). Some linguists include morphology as a branch of syntax. In this book, however, we will look at morphology as the patterns that exist within words, whereas our treatment of syntax will consider whole words and how they form sentences.

By now you should have the "feel" of language, the sense of it as structure. Structure alone, however, does not guarantee effective communication any more than an artist's first sketch on canvas guarantees a good oil painting. The original sketch may be strong, interesting, and full of promise, but the final judgment of the work rests upon the artist's use of his paints.

In the same way, the final appraisal of language depends upon a person's ability to use words to communicate his meaning. When we deal with meaning and how meaning is achieved through language we are looking at yet another aspect of grammar called *semantics* (Gk. σημαίνω, 'I signify'). Semanticists study the many subtle shades of meaning that words and phrases are capable of expressing. They ask: "What did he *really* mean by that?" Of course single, exact, absolute meanings are impossible, especially when values and abstractions are under consideration. "*Exactly* what do you mean?" may be impossible to answer, for an answer must be stated in words, and these words must, in turn, be subject to semantic analysis. Hence the semanticist's work, like the conscientious housewife's, is never done.

Phonology, morphology, syntax, and semantics form the nucleus of linguistics, the central core of language study. Together they constitute the grammar of a language (see fig. 1).

Notice that language exhibits a hierarchical organization in which the units of each level above the first are composed of units from the next lower level. Linguists study the various levels of the hierarchy as well as the intermediate transitions between them. Phonology pertains to the elementary sounds of language (phonemes) and their combinations. Morphology deals with the smallest meaningful units of language (morphemes) and their composition. Syntax looks at the formation of phrases and sentences out of these smaller units. Semantics deals with the meanings of

Figure 1   The Elements of Grammar

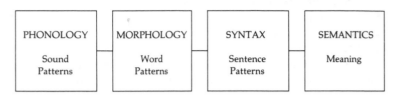

PHONOLOGY	MORPHOLOGY	SYNTAX	SEMANTICS
Sound Patterns	Word Patterns	Sentence Patterns	Meaning

morphemes and words and the various ways in which meanings of larger units are constructed. The intermediate transitions between these levels are made according to orderly patterns or rules. As we study these patterns, we discover that language is a system so organized that by learning a manageable set of elements and the rules for their combination, we can produce an indefinite variety of particular messages. It is this flexibility that gives language its preeminent position among the various means of communication.

As students of Greek you are working hard to learn how to handle with skill and assurance the grammar of New Testament Greek. It will be a long and rigorous apprenticeship. But from that labor will emerge something every student must have to be able to interpret the New Testament correctly: a sense of structure. Then, and only then, will you be ready to pursue that elusive thing called "exegesis."

Historical Linguistics

Like people, languages have individual histories. English, for example, can be traced back to Old English, commonly called Anglo-Saxon, which in turn can be traced back to an ancient language known as Proto-Germanic. Such gradual alteration goes largely unnoticed by the speakers of the language. Yet one glance at the works of Chaucer shows how much English has changed in a relatively short time.

It is this type of historical study with which historical linguists are concerned. Using the tools of descriptive linguistics, they analyze languages on the basis of grammar and trace the historical development of their sound systems, vocabularies, and writing systems. The present book seeks not merely to describe Greek as it was spoken and written in the first century A.D., that is, during the New Testament period, but to show how its sounds, forms, and constructions developed from older stages of the language and ultimately from a linguistic ancestor that gave rise to a wide range of languages, including English.

Comparative Linguistics

Just as there are individual languages, so there are language "families" all over the world. Such families have common characteristics, just as there would be among close relatives. By comparing the structures of various languages, which individually are the concern of descriptive linguistics, the comparative linguist can show the relationships between languages. For example, comparative linguists might investigate how the sound system of English compares with that of French, how the morphology of German is similar to or different from that of Dutch, or how Greek writing compares with that of Russian. Whereas the comparative study of English and French might show more similarities than differences of meaning and structure, the comparative study of English and a language from some totally different family, such as Hebrew, would be concerned largely with differences.

The comparative method is important because it allows us to establish relationships among languages, common ancestors for different languages, and patterns of historical development. Careful investigation of ancient Greek has revealed many similarities between this language and both Latin and Sanskrit (an ancient language of India). Greek is also a relative of English, though perhaps you are not yet aware of this relationship. Comparative linguistics will give you a better understanding of both the similarities and differences between your own language and that of the New Testament.

In addition to the main branches mentioned above, linguistics includes many other important disciplines. *Graphemics*, the study of writing systems, and *orthography* (spelling) are important branches of descriptive linguistics. *Transformational-generative grammar* tries to encapsulate a speaker's knowledge of his language by generating all the possible sentences in that language. *Applied linguistics* is a broad category that includes computer languages, speech and hearing therapies, mathematical linguistics, some types of animal communication research, and a number of other highly specialized activities. *Psycholinguistics* studies the relationship between language and the mind, while *sociolinguistics* looks at the relationship between language and society. *Lexicology* deals with the development of valid principles and methods of word study, while *lexicography* applies these to the study of individual words. Finally, *etymology* is a branch of lexicography that studies the origins and derivations of words.

It is obvious that linguistics is in a well-developed stage today, as far as methodology is concerned. We should not be disturbed to find so many different and sometimes competing linguistic activities. This is the hallmark of a living, vigorous, and growing science. In subsequent chapters we will be discussing each of the basic components of linguistic analysis in considerable detail, starting with the phonological component because it is in some ways the simplest to describe and because it can be used to introduce many basic linguistic concepts. However, to set the scene for our dual purpose of discussing both what the linguistic study of the Greek language involves and also how it can contribute to your analysis of the New Testament, first we must describe some of the basic characteristics of human language in general, and of the linguist's approach to it.

How Does Linguistics Differ from Traditional Grammar?

Although no sharp dividing line exists between traditional and linguistic grammars, linguistics differs from traditional grammar in several basic ways.

It Is Scientific

The most important claim linguists make is that their approach to the study of language is scientific. To be scientific a study should be *empirical*, *exact*, and, therefore, *objective*. Restricting evidence to what can be seen or heard is another way of saying that the scientific method is empirical. This requires objective communication about the subject under study, because it is easier to make two people see the same thing than to make them think or feel the same way about it. Because it uses the empirical approach, the scientific method is also exact. Instead of saying that the sun is hot, the scientist measures the degree of heat by means of a thermometer. Instead of subjectively declaring that a stone is heavy, the scientist counts the number of weights required to balance the object on a scale. Such measurements as described above can often be stated in mathematical terms. Likewise many linguists have found that the use of mathematical terms is the most precise way to describe the functions of language.

As the scientific study of language, linguistics also tries to be objective. There is no place in science for culturally or emotionally based views of language. People who regard Italian as "musical," French as "flowing," or German as "guttural" reveal much about their understanding of language. Such notions are often just as vague as those of the Spanish emperor Charles V, for whom English was the proper language for commerce, German for warfare, French for women, Italian for friends, and Spanish for God. The layman's description of German as "guttural" actually tells us more about him than about the German language. The linguist's description of this language in terms of the various movements of the jaw, tongue, lips, and throat is far more explicit and informative.

As a science, the goal of linguistics is to observe and to describe the subconscious knowledge all speakers have of their own native languages. But linguistics does not consist merely of the observation and description of language. Every scientist, including the linguistic scientist, seeks to discover the general principles that underlie the variety of observable facts. In the long run, a "universal grammar" (if one could ever be written) is the most important task of linguistics. Yet even if such a goal proves to be unattainable, we are likely to learn an enormous amount about language in the course of the scientific quest.

It Is Descriptive

In the second place, linguistics is concerned with what *is* said, not what *ought* to be said. In other words, it describes language without attempting to prescribe rules of correctness. For the linguist, there is no absolute or infallible correctness in language. Thus if people say "ain't," a linguist considers it his duty to record the fact. He is an observer and recorder of facts, not a judge.

A simple illustration of how this principle applies to the New Testament will indicate how the linguist approaches language descriptively. Many readers have cringed at the Greek of Revelation 1:4: ἀπὸ ὁ ὢν καὶ ὁ ἦν καὶ ὁ ἐρχόμενος ("From the one who is and who was and who is coming"). From a purely objective point of view, there is nothing wrong with this phrase. It conveys its meaning clearly, and the communication of meaning is, after all, the purpose of language. Why, then, do some people reject the utterance as "bad" Greek? The answer lies in the rule of Greek grammar that says the genitive case is to be used in constructions following the preposition ἀπό. Subjected to this rule, the phrase in Revelation 1:4 is a "prohibited" form, since the words that follow ἀπό are in the "wrong" (nominative) case.

Actually the expression is quite normal—and therefore perfectly grammatical—for people such as the Jews who often regarded God's name as indeclinable. Had the Greek contained quotation marks, the usage would never have been questioned. If, for example, I were to say, "The Constitution of the United States guarantees liberty to 'we the people,'" every American would understand the allusion to the Preamble to the Constitution, even though someone who had never heard of the Preamble might be horrified at the use of the "wrong" pronoun after the preposition *to*. In cases such as these, the linguist's task is to describe the phenomenon and, if he can, to account for it in some way using a general theory. Judgments about "correct" and "incorrect" language are always social, human decisions about the desirability of utterances. But there is nothing in the utterances themselves, as sounds we hear or as words we read, that brands them as "right" or "wrong."

It Emphasizes the Spoken Language

A final way in which linguistics differs from traditional grammar is that linguistics regards the *spoken* language as primary, not the written. Writing is merely a form of talk—talk that has been caught in flight and pinned down on paper so that the words can be *heard* (not merely seen) again.

Most of our schooling, with its necessary attention to books and writing, makes it difficult for us to recognize the primacy of speech. Moreover, since the written representation of language is all that we can deal with in the case of the New Testament, it is easy to overlook the basic phenomenon of speech. But even if you have never heard a word of spoken Greek, you can recognize that the language of the New Testament is essentially "recorded speech." It differs from the artificial literary Greek of such contemporary first-century authors as Diodorus, Strabo, Plutarch, and Philo. So by regarding language primarily as sound we can learn to appreciate the fact that the language of the New Testament was the common speech of everyday life.

How Do Linguists Characterize Language?

We have defined linguistics as a scientific discipline that describes language in all its aspects and formulates theories as to how it works. But what exactly *is* language? How does one define it? What are its characteristic features? One of the best ways to answer these questions is to see how linguists have described the essential features of human language.

Sounds

Except for sign languages, language is composed of meaningful *sounds*. Until recently the written form of language was emphasized more than the spoken form. But the fact remains that the primary and by far most widespread means of human communication is speech. It is therefore legitimate for the linguist to be primarily concerned with speech and only secondarily concerned with writing (as a more or less faithful reflection of speech).

Linear

Another fundamental feature of language is that it is *linear*. Since the sounds of language are produced by successive movements of the speech organs, we can accurately represent language by using separate symbols for each distinct sound. These symbols may then be arranged in a linear succession that parallels the order in which the sounds are produced. The order of the symbols is irrelevant: in English we are accustomed to a left-to-right order, but any other sequence would do. At first the Greeks wrote from right to left, as did the Phoenicians, from whom they adopted their alphabet. Later the Greeks wrote alternately from right to left and from left to right. This method of writing was called βουστροφηδόν ("as oxen turn at the plow"). This may have been an effective working procedure, but it was tough on the reader. Standard left-to-right writing was established during the classical period and adopted subsequently by all who borrowed from the Greeks.

Arbitrary

Because there is no natural or necessary connection between a word and the thing or idea it is communicating, language is also said to be *arbitrary*. The English word *baby* may be expressed by quite different sounding words in other languages (cf. German *Kind*, Spanish *criatura*, or French *enfant*). If there had to a direct connection between the nature of things and the expressions used to represent them, there could only be one language.

A special class of words seems to invalidate this statement. They are called *onomatopoeic* words, words that imitate the sounds of their referents, such as *bang, boom, clang, clatter, splash, swish*, and so on. But apart from instances of exceptional identity (e.g., English *meow*, French *miaou*, and German *miau*), identical meanings in different languages are never expressed by means of the same sound sequence. Thus Japanese cars go *boo-boo*, Hungarian roosters go *kukoriku*, and French cats purr by saying *ronron*.

The arbitrary nature of language also suggests that change is normal and to be expected. New products often require the invention of new words or shifts in the meanings of other words. When man invented an undersea vehicle, he coined a new word, *submarine* (*sub*, meaning "under," and *marine*, connoting water [Lat. *mare*, 'sea']). The word *television* has a similar history of coinage: a Latin base (*video*, 'I see') with a Greek prefix (τηλε, 'distant'). Changes also occur when words are discarded from language: we seldom speak today of *parlors* or *cellars*. Sometimes the choice of a word is motivated by cultural reasons, as when the British adopted the Norman word *beef* for a type of meat rather than its Anglo-Saxon equivalent *cow*. The point is that no word is "ordained," nor is one word superior to another.

Conventional and Systematic

Only when we consider an item of language in isolation does it become arbitrary. Otherwise language is *conventional*, with regular and specific patterns, which makes it possible for us to learn and use a foreign language such as Greek.

Because language is conventional, it is also *systematic*: it can be described in terms of a finite number of linguistic units that can combine only in a limited number of ways. That is to say, languages have their own phonological, morphological, and syntactical systems, each with its own rules of permissible combination and order. The grammar of a language, as we have seen, is concerned with the description, analysis, and formalization of these linguistic patterns. Linguists are constantly searching for satisfactory ways of describing these rules and patterns, and in many respects they have developed more precise and rigorous methods and attained more definitive results than have traditional grammarians.

Unique

Since languages are arbitrary, conventional means of communication, each language must deservedly be considered *unique*, both in its inventory of sounds and in the manner in which these are used to form meaningful sentences. This means that every language will have its own peculiarities. To learn a foreign language, you have of course to be able to accept and understand these differences. In German there are those irksome cases: the shop is *der Laden*, but you go into *den Laden*, and once inside you are in *dem Laden*, which is all very confusing to the native English speaker. Then we have the word order: there is a popular (but mistaken) idea that German sentences are spoken and written backwards! On the other hand, the difficulty of Greek to most beginners is not the script (which is fascinating if thoroughly mastered at the beginning) or the syntax (which does, however, have cases), but the large variety of verb forms and the number of so-called *irregular verbs*. When studying a foreign language, do not be concerned if some aspect of grammar is not immediately clear to you. What may appear difficult at first will become easier as the language becomes more familiar.

Similar

Despite the differences in grammatical systems alluded to above, all languages have certain features in common. Since language is composed of sounds and has a linear pattern, all linguistic units will be stated basically in terms of sounds and sound sequences. Since language is arbitrary, the connection between sound and meaning will always be indirect. Since language is conventional and systematic, there will always be certain patterns of sounds and sound sequences. Since language is unique, there will always be new patterns to learn in the study of foreign languages.

Most importantly, because languages are similar, all languages will share the same high degree of adequacy in communication— in spite of their differences. Linguists reject the notion that any one language can be more expressive than all other languages, an opinion incorrectly held by many teachers of New Testament

Greek. God has undoubtedly conferred special honor upon Greek as the language chosen for the inscripturation of the New Testament, but Greek is not inherently superior to the other languages of the world. At present, both linguists and Bible translators agree that any language can express whatever ideas its speakers are capable of having, and that a language can and does expand and change to fit new needs or ideas those speakers may have.

The similarities between languages permit us to posit certain universal features common to the grammars of all languages. But these features are of an abstract nature, embedded in what linguists call the *deep structure*. The more obvious features of the grammars of different languages, those that are on the "surface" (such as the order of words or the formation of plurals), vary from language to language. Traditional grammar books of foreign languages often make the mistake of assuming that all languages have the same surface grammar (usually Latin or Greek grammar). In this spirit grammarians often remark that English is defective in the middle voice—all respectable languages, it would seem, must have the middle voice! But to expect English or any other language to follow Greek in this respect is simply preposterous.

How Is Linguistics Related to Other Fields?

Just as we felt it necessary to determine the place of language in the total scheme of things, so it seems wise at this point to place linguistics among the other branches of study. Language is such a universal and multipurpose form of human behavior that it turns up as part, at least, of the subject matter of many other disciplines besides linguistics. Therefore, before we close this rather lengthy introduction to our subject, we should take note of the practical applications of linguistics.

Anthropology

Anthropologists and linguists have long enjoyed close ties with each other, especially in the United States. Much of the work in linguistics during the early part of this century grew out of a necessity for understanding the languages of various American Indian communities. These and many other exotic tongues proved to be very different from the European languages so cherished by scholars of the nineteenth century. Hence linguists had to devise new techniques of linguistic analysis to describe the languages of the Americas, Southwest Asia, and the Pacific islands.

The anthropologist becomes interested in linguistics if only because he must frequently overcome the language barrier before being able to analyze a given culture. Having surmounted that barrier, he is nevertheless likely to continue to treat language as an integral part of culture and to inquire into possible interrelations between language and cultural patterns.

Philosophy

What language is and how it functions are also important philosophical concerns. Some philosophers have addressed the metaphysical implications of language, while others are interested in determining the relationship between language and logic. Still others are interested in linguistics for its insights into language acquisition. Philosophical linguists wonder how a question like "Have you beaten your wife lately?" achieves its ambiguity, or how the word *table* can appear to have distinctly different meanings (e.g., "water table," "dining table," or "table an amendment"). To answer these questions intelligently requires a sophisticated understanding of language.

Psychology

For the psychologist, linguistics provides a wealth of information for the investigation of human nature. *Psycholinguistics* brings together the theoretical and empirical tools of both psychology and linguistics in order to study the underlying knowledge and ability that people must have in order to use language effectively. The psychologist is frequently interested in the application of linguistics to a particular area of psychology. The general or theoretical psychologist is drawn to linguistics when he tries to describe and explain human behavior in terms of speech and language. The social psychologist is interested in linguistics because of the importance he ascribes to language in social interaction. The child psychologist meets problems related to language in studying the development of language and speech in the child. The abnormal psychologist and the psychiatrist encounter problems of language in studying aphasia (the loss or impairment of the ability to speak) and the distorted speech of psychotics. This list might also include the speech pathologist and other professionals who are concerned with the education of the deaf and blind. Linguists and psychologists share so many interests in language that psycholinguistics is rapidly becoming one of the major branches of present-day American linguistics.

Sociology

Linguists are not interested in producing a prescriptive grammar that is designed and used to alter actual language by prohibiting certain forms. They do recognize, however, that differences exist in language use, and that some usages are associated with members of particular social classes or geographic regions. The field of *sociolinguistics* is devoted to the investigation and explanation of the social factors that lead to this diversity.

The most extensive work in sociolinguistics has treated the problem of social dialects—differences in language use due to differences in social context. Whereas in traditional grammar anything that smacks of informality tends to be avoided, the sociolinguist attempts to take account of the different levels of formality without selecting some levels as "right" and others as "wrong." An example is the English rule that requires the use of *whom* and not *who* as the relative pronoun in a sentence like "the man _____ you saw was my friend." In an informal conversation, the colloquial *who* would be acceptable, while on a formal occasion the more acceptable way of making the point would be to use *whom*. The difference is one of formality and not of correct usage.

Sociolinguists do not determine which level of language is the best for society. Since 1635 the French Academy has had the right to decide what is and what is not permissible in the French language. The authority for determining the "correct" forms for English resides primarily in grammar books. Normative English grammar teaches us to say "It is I" instead of "It's me," to avoid ending sentences with prepositions, to use "each other" instead of "one another" when only two people are involved, and so on. But what is correct and what is incorrect is ultimately a matter of what is accepted by society. If everyone says "It's me," then "It's me" is correct English, regardless of what the grammar books say.

Biblical Studies

In general, studies of the biblical languages have been marked by frequent failure to take proper account of the methods and results of linguistic science. But it is also true that few linguists are acquainted with the biblical languages and have thus been somewhat handicapped in their attempts to apply linguistics to the Bible. In the last two or three decades, however, there have been a number of signs of increasing communication between linguists and biblical scholars. *Biblical linguistics* is beginning to emerge as one of the most fundamental disciplines in biblical studies—as important, for example, as the study of molecular physics in the natural sciences. Recently, biblical scholars have become concerned with the problems of language to a degree only equaled in the early history of modern comparative linguistics, when scholars such as Deissmann and Moulton began demolishing the myth of the privileged position of "Holy Ghost" Greek. And today this group is being augmented by several individuals who are specifically interested in what they call *the semantics of biblical language.*

What the future holds is difficult to predict. Until recently, publishers had been slow in presenting scientific concepts of Greek grammar because so many teachers were dedicated to the traditional approach. New Testament scholars were reluctant to teach, or even learn, the new grammar until textbooks were available. In recent years, however, many linguistically oriented books have been published covering everything from discourse analysis to lexical semantics. Some are actually traditional grammar texts with some of the "new" terminology added to give the impression of being up-to-date. Others are truly integrated with the work being done in linguistics. With still others, linguistics has become a sort of academic status symbol, pursued with the same blind devotion that traditional grammarians lavish on "It is I."

But one thing is certain: today's Greek student stands at the crossroads. With the tools of modern language research available for the first time, a serious reappraisal of the traditional approach to Greek grammar is underway. If the student of the New Testament is to become something more than a well-trained technician, he must sooner or later develop a solid perspective on linguistic study and on the nature of language itself.

This book is aimed at developing such a perspective. Let us not get discouraged if the process takes longer than expected or desired. Language was not made by linguists, but by humble people like you and me. It is the most democratic thing we have. Hence all the ideas underlying linguistics are simple and well within the grasp of anyone who will take the trouble to think.

Suggestions for Further Reading

Of the many popular introductions to the study of language crowding our library shelves today, the following books will give the interested newcomer the best overview of linguistics in general and some details of specific modern linguistic schools in particular.

Bodmer, Frederick. *The Loom of Language*. New York: Norton, 1944.
Dineen, Francis P. *An Introduction to General Linguistics*. New York: Holt, Rinehart & Winston, 1967.
Gaeng, Paul A. *Introduction to the Principles of Language*. New York: Harper & Row, 1971.
Hall, Robert. *Linguistics and Your Language*. Garden City, N.Y.: Doubleday, 1960.
Pei, Mario. *Invitation to Linguistics: A Basic Introduction to the Science of Language*. Chicago: Regnery, 1965.
Wardhaugh, Ronald. *Introduction to Linguistics*. New York: McGraw-Hill, 1972.

On the wave of interest in linguistics on the part of biblical scholars, several writers have attempted to explain what has been happening. The following is a brief list of articles that cover the various ways in which linguistics can serve the Bible student.

Erickson, Richard J. "Linguistics and Biblical Language: A Wide-Open Field." *Journal of the Evangelical Theological Society* 26 (1983):257–63.
_____. "Some Recent Contributions to Biblical Linguistics." *Theological Students' Fellowship Bulletin* (March–April 1985):23–24.
Gleason, H. A. "Linguistics in the Service of the Church." *Hartford Quarterly* 1 (1961):7–27.
_____. "Some Contributions of Linguistics to Biblical Studies." *Hartford Quarterly* 4 (1963):47–56.
Nida, Eugene A. "Implications of Contemporary Linguistics for Biblical Scholarship." *Journal of Biblical Literature* 91 (1972):73–89.
_____. "Linguistic Theories and Bible Translating." *The Bible Translator* 23 (1972):301–8.
Schmidt, Daryl D. "The Study of Hellenistic Greek Grammar in the Light of Contemporary Linguistics." *Perspectives in Religious Studies* 11 (1984):27–38.
Smalley, W. A. "The Place of Linguistics in Bible Translation." *The Bible Translator* 16 (1965):105–12.
Taber, Charles R. "Exegesis and Linguistics." *The Bible Translator* 20 (1969):150–53.

2

Phonology: The Sounds of Greek

Language as Sound

Linguistics, as we have seen, is concerned primarily with the spoken word. For all known human languages, sound is the concrete means of expression. More than two thousand of the world's languages have no writing system, but all have a sound system.

Phonology is the branch of linguistics that deals with speech sounds. It consists of the related studies of phonetics and phonemics. *Phonetics* involves the analysis and description of speech sounds per se, encompassing two major areas of investigation. *Acoustic phonetics* deals with the physics of the sound waves themselves, which are usually studied with the help of special machinery that produces *spectrograms*, graphic representations of the sound patterns.

Articulatory phonetics is the study of how various sounds are produced by the organs of speech. The speech organs include the lungs, the trachea, the larynx, the pharynx, the nose, and the mouth. The term *vocal tract* is used to refer collectively to the throat, nose, and mouth.

Because phonetics is basically concerned with the description of human speech sounds, it can most effectively be discussed in terms of the vocal tract. To try to describe what takes place in the vocal tract is a little like trying to describe what it is like to be happy. Words and symbols are only substitutes. Nevertheless, poets and philosophers have been talking about happiness since the dawn of literature, and linguists have developed a system of phonetic classification that makes it possible for us to discuss speech sounds objectively and accurately.

As the study of human speech sounds, phonetics is useful to a linguist—even though it provides only basic background knowledge. Phonetics is the prelude to *phonemics*, the study of a language as a system of sounds that can be used by speakers of that language to effect communication. It is this knowledge of the systematic ways in which sounds are put together in a language that enables a speaker to form meaningful utterances, to invent new words, to recognize "accents," and so forth. This system is known as the phonemic system. Here, as in morphology and syntax, linguists look for the systematic patterning that is characteristic of all human language.

In this chapter we will look at the sounds and sound system of Greek, attempting to become aware of the various ways in which language sounds can be produced, how these sounds are organized into a system, and how a knowledge of phonology can help us become better students of New Testament Greek. In order to understand the phonology of Greek, however, we must first have some knowledge of the process by which human language activity takes place.

The Speech Process

The essence of speech is the act of communication between two people, one who creates sounds and another who hears them and finds them meaningful. To illustrate this speaking circuit between people, let us use the model proposed by Saussure (see fig. 2).

Figure 2   The Speech Process

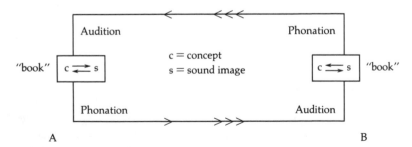

Suppose that speaker A desires to convey a message—in this case, the concept *book*—to hearer B, who uses the same language. To do this, A's brain must first translate this concept (c) into the appropriate sound image (s), made up of a set of sounds that are arbitrarily used to convey this concept. This purely psychological process—involving the kind of nonvocal sound symbols we use when we talk to ourselves without moving our lips or tongues—is immediately followed by a physiological response to a nerve impulse from the brain. It is this nerve impulse that causes the organs of speech to produce the sound sequence that A wishes to convey to B. Saussure called this response the action of *phonation*—that is, the production of speech sounds by the vocal organs. Air that is forced from the lungs and shaped into the desired sounds by the vocal tract is propelled from the mouth or nose as sound waves that reach the hearer's ear. At this point, which Saussure called the point of *audition*, the order is reversed. By a physiological process the sound waves caused by the sound sequence (in this case the sound in *book*) are transmitted to B's brain, which, in turn, translates the audible sound symbols into the appropriate sound image (s). Finally, B decodes the message by associating the sound image with the corresponding concept (c). Since A and B speak the same language, A's concept will more or less coincide with B's.

Having briefly sketched the speech process, let us now take a closer look at the speech sounds themselves, with the view of describing them, classifying them, and finally, examining how they function in the Greek language.

Phonetics: How Sounds Are Made

Human beings are equipped with certain physical characteristics that make the activities of breathing, sucking, biting, chewing, and swallowing possible. Essentially the same parts of the anatomy that participate in these functions also serve as the vocal tract, the sound-producing mechanism. A knowledge of this mechanism is essential to an understanding of the *articulation*, or production, of all speech sounds.

The Human Vocal Apparatus

One can regard the group of human organs that produce speech as a wind instrument such as a clarinet. Most speech

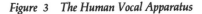

Figure 3   The Human Vocal Apparatus

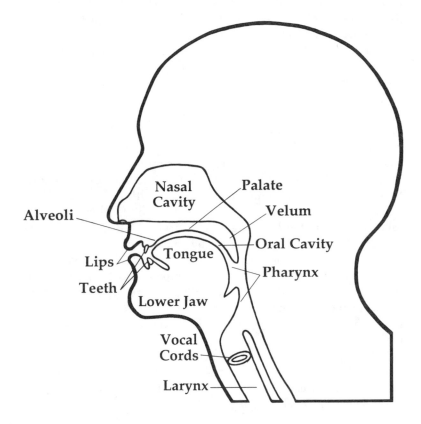

sounds—all of them in English and Greek—are produced by a stream of air that begins in the lungs and is forced out of the mouth or nose. Referring to figure 3, we can trace the route of air as it is forced by the diaphragm and rib muscles out of the lungs into the trachea, or windpipe. When it reaches the top of the trachea, the air passes through the larynx, or voice box. To the larynx are fastened the vocal cords—two liplike tissues that may or may not vibrate as the air passes through them. The air stream then passes through the pharynx, or back of the throat. From here the air either enters the nasal cavity and escapes through nostrils, or it enters the oral cavity and escapes through the teeth and lips. As the air stream moves through the oral cavity, it passes over a muscle called the tongue and below the roof of the mouth—

made up, in order from the rear, of the nonbony part called the velum; of the hard, bony part called the palate; and of the ridge formed by the roots of the upper teeth called the gums or alveoli. The lower jaw is also included as a speech organ since it determines whether the oral cavity is large or small when the air stream passes through.

The Articulation of Consonants

To understand how the individual sounds of Greek are formed, we can begin with the factors involved in the formation of consonants. These factors, each having to do with the vocal tract, can be put as three questions: (1) Do the vocal cords vibrate?; (2) To what extent is the air flow restricted?; and (3) Where do the lips or tongue touch or approach other organs? In discussing these questions, keep in mind that the letters of the Greek alphabet do not, and probably never did, exactly represent the basic phonemes of Greek. Linguists have therefore developed an international phonetic alphabet that attempts to indicate each speech sound using a different symbol.*

1. Do the vocal cords vibrate?

When you make a z sound, you can feel the buzzing made by the vibrating vocal cords by holding your Adam's apple or by putting your hands on top of your head. You can even hum a tune (if you can hum a tune), since the stream of air coming from the lungs consists, in large part, of regular musical waves. Now switch to an s sound. Even though your lips and teeth remain in the same position, you will feel no buzzing, nor will you be able to hum, for the vocal cords are not vibrating. The essential difference between these two sounds is that in the production of z the vocal cords vibrate whereas in the production of s they do not. Thus z is called a *voiced* sound, s a *voiceless* sound.

The vibration or lack of vibration of the vocal cords also distinguishes the members of the following pairs in English. The first sound in each pair is voiced; the second sound is voiceless. (Don't take my word for it. Practice hearing and feeling the buzz.)

---

* For those who are interested, a number of textbooks on the subject are recommended in the bibliography to this chapter. However, since phonetic symbols make a text more difficult to read, this book uses the conventional written letters, even though it is the spoken form that is being discussed. Also, in what follows I am following the standard American pronunciation of the Greek letters.

v and f
b and p
d and t
g and k

For some of the voiced sounds, especially b, d, and g, it is more difficult to observe the vibration as these sounds cannot be prolonged. Nevertheless, if you hold your Adam's apple with all five fingers, you will feel your throat tighten for voiced b but remain relaxed for voiceless p. The same observation can be made for voiced d and g, and voiceless t and k.

While vowels in English are regularly voiced, consonants may be either voiced or voiceless. Greek consonants, too, may be divided into two groups according to the tension or slackness of the vocal cords:

Voiced: β, γ, δ, λ, ρ, μ, ν, nasal-γ (before κ, γ, χ, ξ), ζ, and consonantal ι and υ.
Voiceless: π, κ, τ, φ, χ, θ, σ, ψ, and ξ.

2. *To what extent is the air flow restricted?*

Two answers to this question are possible—completely or incompletely. If the restriction is complete, the air stream stops. If the restriction is incomplete, the air stream continues. This distinction provides the basis for a classification of consonants into stops and continuants.

A *stop*, as the name suggests, is a sound in which the air stream is completely restricted or interrupted. It is difficult to locate the voiced quality in b, d, and g; we can say "babababa," but we cannot say "bbbbbb." Thus:

β, δ, γ are voiced stops.
π, τ, κ are voiceless stops.

Linguists also refer to these sounds as *plosives*, since the breath, which has temporarily been compressed, escapes upon release with a mild explosion.

In contrast to the six Greek stops above, *continuants*, in sounds like μ, φ, and σ, do not completely restrict or interrupt the air stream at any time. You can articulate them continually, until you are out of breath if you wish. The fact that you can continue makes the word *continuant* an appropriate term for such sounds.

According to the degree of obstruction of the air stream, starting with those sounds that show the greatest amount, we may distinguish three types of continuants.

First are the *nasal continuants*. When the velum is open, the air stream enters the nasal cavity. The initial sounds in *mad* and *no* and the final sound in *ring* differ in articulation from those in *bad*, *dough*, and *rig* only insofar as during their enunciation the nasal passage is kept open for the air to issue through the nose. Since the air escapes from the nasal cavity rather than from between the lips, the sounds are termed *nasal continuants*. In Greek the three letters μ, ν, and nasal-γ are voiced nasal continuants. All other sounds in Greek are typically oral—that is, the air escapes from the oral cavity.

The *lateral continuants* are the second type of continuants. When you make an *l* sound, the tip of the tongue touches the gums (alveoli). The sides of the tongue do not. The air stream passes over one or both sides of the tongue on its way to the outside. Since *lateral* is another word for *side* (Lat. *latus*), *l* is termed a *lateral*. In Greek, λ is the sole voiced lateral continuant.

The *fricative continuants* constitute the third type. The initial sounds of *fine, vine, thigh, thy, seal, zeal,* and *ship*, as well as the medial sound in *pleasure*, are characterized by "noises" (irregular sound waves). The noise is caused by friction. This friction, in turn, is caused by the narrowness of the passageway through which the air stream passes. Because of this friction, the sounds are called fricative continuants (Lat. *frico*, 'I rub').

The Greek fricatives are φ, θ, σ, χ, and ' (the rough breathing). Sometimes the *s*-like sound of σ is called a *sibilant* because of the accompanying hissing noise (Lat. *sibilo*, 'I hiss'). We do not need this label, however, to distinguish the sound. Thus:

φ, θ, σ, χ, ' are voiceless fricative continuants.

It would be nice if the division of consonants into stops and continuants took care of all consonants in Greek. Unfortunately, it does not. One type of sound, for example, consists of a stop and a continuant pushed together into what amounts to a single sound, as in the final sound of *taps*. In a second type, the air stream is never completely interrupted as with a stop, nor can the sound be indefinitely continued as with a continuant.

An *affricate* results from a consonant sound that combines the properties of a stop and a fricative (Lat. *affrico*, 'I rub against'). An affricate is made by cutting off the air flow completely, as in a stop, then releasing it through a very small opening, as in a fricative. The "stop + continuant" of an affricate will be clear to you if you contrast the initial sounds of ψεύδω ("I lie") and σώζω ("I save"). If you prolong the initial sound of both words, you will hear the continuant s. Yet the initial sounds are obviously different. Pronouncing the words slowly and carefully will reveal the p sound in ψεύδω. Just before the s sound, your lips come together and momentarily stop the air stream. This does not happen with the word σώζω.

The Greek affricates are the *double consonants* ζ, ξ, and ψ, ζ is basically a combination of δ and σ; ξ represents κ and σ; and ψ combines π and σ. As with stops, affricates can be either voiced or voiceless. Hence:

> ζ is a voiced affricate.
>
> ξ, ψ are voiceless affricates.

If an affricate is composed of a stop followed by a sibilant, it is called an *assibilate*. The Greek affricates, being combinations of certain consonants and σ, are all assibilates.

Glides (neither stops nor continuants) could also be termed *transitional sounds* since they are characterized by a moving, rather than a stationary, tongue position as they pass to and from the place of articulation. For example, when we pronounce *w* as in *watch*, we cannot continue the *w* sound indefinitely, as with s or v. It inevitably becomes something else—in English, a vowel. Thus in pronouncing *wait, win, wax,* and *we,* the vowel-like quality of *w* is borne out by the fact that there is no stoppage or noticeable friction in its pronunciation; yet it cannot be classified as a vowel because it never forms a syllable center (as vowels do, by definition). In short, *w* is a voiced glide.

Now contrast the following pairs:

am	yam
owl	yowl
ale	Yale
ooze	use (vb.)
who	hue

Precise pronunciation of the above indicates that the *y* sounds in the words in the second column are pronounced, like *w*, as the speech organs move, beginning in one position, then moving toward another (vowel) position. Thus *y*, like *w*, is a voiced glide.

Because they are always found in association with a vowel, though functioning as consonants on account of their nonsyllabic nature, these glides are also known as *semivowels* or *semiconsonants*. They could just as well be called *nonsyllabic vowels* because their role in language is to help in the formation of vowel sequences called *diphthongs* (see pp. 37–38).

The Greek letters ι and υ are sometimes called glides or semivowels because, in addition to representing vowel sounds, they can represent the consonantal sounds *y* (as in *yam*) and *w* (as in *wait*). In this case they are designated ι̯ and υ̯. Consonantal υ̯ was represented by the letter ϝ (digamma) in early Greek. While consonantal ι̯ and υ̯ do not appear in New Testament Greek, their presence often makes itself felt in various phonetic changes. The letter ρ is also classified as a glide, although the sound of *r* (in any language) is probably the most difficult to classify. Hence:

ι̯, υ̯, ρ are voiced glides (or semivowels).

3. *Where do the lips and tongue touch or approach other organs?*

The place where the lips and tongue touch or approach other speech organs is termed the *point of articulation*. In discussing the point of articulation, let us start from the outside, where we can most readily see what happens.

When you pronounce β, π, and μ the two lips touch each other. An adjective derived from a Latin term for "two lips" is *bilabial*. Therefore:

β is a voiced bilabial stop.
π is a voiceless bilabial stop.
μ is a voiced bilabial nasal continuant.

The word *bilabial* now distinguishes the sound of β from the two other voiced stops in Greek, δ and γ; the sound of π from the other voiceless stops, τ and κ; and the sound of μ from the other nasal continuants, ν and nasal-γ. Consequently, β, π, and μ are distinguished from all other sounds in Greek.

In pronouncing the fricative φ you touch the lower lip against the upper teeth and blow the air through whatever space the shape of the teeth permits. For the adjective *lip-tooth* we substitute the Latin equivalent *labiodental*. Thus:

φ is a voiceless labiodental fricative continuant.

The fricative θ is articulated when the tip of the tongue touches or is just below the edge of the upper teeth. The tip of the tongue is, in effect, between the teeth. The Latin equivalent for "between the teeth" is *interdental*. Hence:

θ is a voiceless interdental fricative continuant.

Pronounce δ, τ, and ν. Can you feel the tongue press against the alveoli? The alveoli give us the term *alveolar*. Thus:

δ is a voiced alveolar stop.
τ is a voiceless alveolar stop.
ν is a voiced alveolar nasal continuant.

Now pronounce λ. Notice that the tongue touches the alveoli just behind the front teeth. It does not, however, touch the alveoli toward the sides of the oral cavity (a fact covered by the term *lateral*). Hence:

λ is a voiced alveolar lateral continuant.

When you pronounce σ, however, the situation is somewhat the reverse of that for λ. The tongue presses against the upper teeth (and alveoli) all along the oral cavity except in front. The air stream is channeled through a deep groove down the middle of the tongue. Consequently:

σ is a voiceless deep-groove alveolar fricative continuant.

The glide ι̯ begins with the front part of the tongue close to the palate. This glide, therefore, is differentiated from the others by the term *palatal*:

ι̯ is a voiced palatal glide (or semivowel).

In the articulation for the alveolar sound, the tip of the tongue is high in the oral cavity, hidden from head-on view by the front upper teeth. Now pronounce γ, κ, and nasal-γ. Notice that the tip of the tongue is down near the lower teeth, whereas the back part of the tongue is high and pushed up against the rear part of the palate or against the velum. This articulation is identified by the term *velar*. Hence:

γ is a voiced velar stop.
κ is a voiceless velar stop.
nasal-γ is a voiced velar nasal continuant.

The fricative ʽ (the rough breathing) is somewhat noisier than mere breathing. The friction causes the noise when the air stream hits the relaxed vocal cords or the walls of the pharynx. From the name for the opening between the vocal cords, glottis, the term *glottal* is derived. Thus:

ʽ is a voiceless glottal fricative continuant.

The glide ʮ begins with the lips rounded and the tongue tip pulled back. The back of the tongue is consequently pushed up toward the velum. The lips and the velum, which are the distinctive elements, provide the term *labiovelar*:

ʮ is a voiced labiovelar glide (or semivowel).

The Greek ρ, like the English *r*, begets varied descriptions from phoneticians. Most characteristically, however, ρ is formed with the tip of the tongue turned slightly backward and upward toward the front part of the palate. The sides of the tongue touch the back teeth, and the back part of the tongue is considerably higher than the tip. This "turned back" position of the tongue, termed *retroflex*, differentiates ρ from the other glides. Hence:

ρ is a voiced retroflex glide (or semivowel).

The Description of Consonants

Having described the way in which the Greek consonants are articulated, we can list the individual consonants and the definition of each—a sort of shorthand description of what happens when the sound is produced. For convenience in study, the consonants are grouped according to their formation as stops, continuants, affricates, or glides.

Letter and Sound	*Definition*
β as in *bob*	Voiced bilabial stop
δ as in *dad*	Voiced alveolar stop
γ as in *gag*	Voiced velar stop
π as in *pop*	Voiceless bilabial stop

τ	as in *tat*	Voiceless alveolar stop
κ	as in *cook*	Voiceless velar stop
μ	as in *mum*	Voiced bilabial nasal continuant
ν	as in *none*	Voiced alveolar nasal continuant
nasal-γ	as in *sung*	Voiced velar nasal continuant
λ	as in *lull*	Voiced alveolar lateral continuant
φ	as in *fifth*	Voiceless labiodental fricative continuant
θ	as in *thought*	Voiceless interdental fricative continuant
σ	as in *sing*	Voiceless deep-groove alveolar continuant
χ	as in *chemical*	Voiceless velar fricative continuant
ͤ	as in *home*	Voiceless glottal fricative continuant
ζ	as in *adze*	Voiced alveolar affricate (double consonant)
ψ	as in *taps*	Voiceless bilabial affricate (double consonant)
ξ	as in *relax*	Voiceless velar affricate (double consonant)
ι̯	as in *yet*	Voiced palatal glide (semivowel)
υ̯	as in *win*	Voiced labiovelar glide (semivowel)
ρ	as in *rear*	Voiced retroflex glide (semivowel)

Figure 4 is a matrix charting the consonants of Greek. Memorizing this chart is an excellent way to keep in mind the basic facts about each sound. Points of articulation are shown horizontally, while manners of articulation are listed vertically. When you describe consonants, begin by stating whether the articulation is voiced or voiceless, then identify the point of articulation, and finally, the manner.

The Articulation of Vowels

In many ways it is easier to discuss consonant articulation than vowel articulation. We can describe fairly easily what happens in the mouth at the beginning and ending of a word such as *bit*, for there is a noticeable bilabial closure at the beginning and a definite alveolar closure at the end. However, the sound in the middle of the word is much more difficult to describe, and the movements in the mouth are much harder to specify. We must therefore search for those characteristics that are important in the production of vowel sounds, just as we searched for suitable characteristics to describe consonant sounds.

Figure 4   The Greek Consonants

Manner of Articulation		Point of Articulation								
		Bilabial	Labiodental	Interdental	Alveolar	Palatal	Velar	Glottal	Labiovelar	Retroflex
STOPS	Voiced	β			δ		γ			
	Voiceless	π			τ		κ			
CONTINUANTS Nasal	Voiced	μ			ν		nasal-γ			
Lateral	Voiced				λ					
Fricative	Voiceless		φ	θ	σ		χ	·		
AFFRICATES	Voiced					ζ				
	Voiceless	ψ					ξ			
GLIDES	Voiced					ι̯			ʋ	ρ

Vowels, in contrast to consonants, involve not the obstruction but the shaping of the air stream in its passage through the oral cavity. To characterize vowels we therefore need a slightly different method of reference, even though we may still refer to the criteria of manner and place of articulation. For vowels, *manner of articulation* involves voicing, lip rounding or spreading, lengthening, and degree of muscular tension. All languages have voiced vowels. Some, like Japanese, also have voiceless ones. Lip spreading versus rounding is also typical of all languages. Some languages, such as French and German, can distinguish meanings by use of this feature alone. Another difference in the manner of articulation has to do with the lengthening or shortening of vowels depending on the kind of consonants that follow them. Finally, there is a criterion of the tenseness or laxness of the tongue muscles and lower jaw, as seen in the degree of tenseness between the pairs *beat/bit, bait/bet,* and *food/good.*

Place of articulation involves generalizations in relation to the front and back of the mouth, as well as tongue height. We can speak of *high, mid,* and *low vowels,* depending on the relative height of the tongue during vowel production. We can also speak of *front, central,* and *back vowels.* If you start with your tongue forward and fairly close to the roof of your mouth, and slowly lower your tongue and jaw, you will pronounce, in order, ι (as in *beet*), η (as in *babe*), ε (as in *bet*), and finally, with the tongue and jaw in the lowest position, α (as in *pot*). Because of the shape of your mouth, your tongue will be considerably further back than it was for ι by the time you reach α. Move it further back still, and raise your tongue toward the roof of your mouth, and you will pronounce o (as in *bought*), ω (as in *bold*), and υ (as in *boot*). This pattern is the basis for the vowel rectangle pictured in figure 5, which gives a schematic representation of the mouth. (Nobody, of course, has a rectangle in his mouth. The rectangle is merely a graphic device that indicates the relative positions of the tongue and jaw when individual vowels are compared. The rectangle is presented as though it is in the mouth of a person looking to the left-hand margin of the page.)

Figure 5   The Vowel Rectangle

	Front (unrounded)	Central	Back (rounded)
High	ι beet (long) / bit (short)		υ boot (long) / book (short)
Mid	η babe		ω bold
Low	ε bet	α pot (long) / bat (short)	o bought

In pronouncing the various vowels, did you notice anything about the shape of the lips? In forming the back vowels, the lips have been rounded. In forming the front and central vowels, the lips are not rounded. Linguists transfer the terms from the lips to the vowels. In Greek, front and central vowels are *unrounded*. In Greek—but certainly not in French and German—all back vowels and only back vowels are *rounded*. Notice also that only one Greek vowel, α, is in the central position, with the tongue as low as possible. That is why the α sound has been called the "doctor's vowel." When the doctor asks you to say *ah*, he wants a wide-open mouth with the tongue as flat as possible so he can observe your throat.

The Description of Vowels

Just as we listed consonant definitions earlier, we here group the vowels together for convenience of study:

Letter and Sound	Definition
ι as in *beet*	High front unrounded
η as in *babe*	Mid front unrounded
ε as in *bet*	Low front unrounded
α as in *pot*	Low central unrounded
o as in *bought*	Low back rounded
ω as in *bold*	Mid back rounded
υ as in *boot*	High back rounded

Diphthongs

Vowels followed by an upward glide to the front or back in the same syllable are called diphthongs. Diphthongs, as the existence of this special term indicates (Gk. δίφθογγος, 'having two sounds'), are actually halfway between a single sound sequence and a sequence of two sound segments. Pronounce αι (as in *eye*). In a mirror, you can easily see the movement of jaw and tongue as you pronounce the sound. Your jaw and tongue start in the low central position for an α but rapidly glide to or toward the high front position.

A similar diphthong is οι. At the start of the diphthong, the jaw is low (the teeth are apart), the tongue is back, and the lips are rounded. This is, of course, the position for o. Then, in one coordinated movement, the jaw rises to the high position (the teeth come closer together), the tongue moves forward, and the lips are unrounded. A mirror can verify this movement from the low back rounded position to or toward the high front unrounded position. Again, a vowel plus a glide in one syllable has produced a diphthong.

A second type of diphthong can be illustrated by αυ. In pronouncing it, notice carefully the jaw, tongue, and lip movements. For the initial sound, the jaw is low, the tongue flat, and the lips unrounded—in short, the position for α. Then the jaw rises, the tongue moves back, and the lips are rounded—everything moves to or toward the high back rounded position. Once again, the movement in producing αυ is so great that one has no trouble seeing it.

Figure 6   The Greek Diphthongs

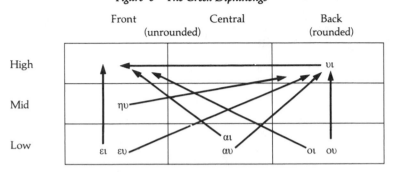

Greek has a large set of such vowels followed by a glide. The diphthongs in Greek are αι, ει, οι, αυ, ευ, ηυ, ου, and υι. Notice that the second vowel is always ι or υ. In some Greek textbooks, ει and ου are labeled *spurious diphthongs* when found in certain words. This means that either of these diphthongs can arise from contraction of vowels or from compensatory lengthening (see p. 44) rather than from the combination of ε + ι and ο + υ. A distinction is also made in some grammars between *proper* and *improper diphthongs*, the latter being those with *iota subscript* (ᾳ, ῃ, ῳ). Again, the terms are not particularly well chosen. Actually, ᾳ, ῃ, and ῳ were no longer diphthongs by New Testament times, but had "monophthongized"— blended into a single vowel sound (Gk. μόνος, 'one,' + φθόγγος, 'sound')—and so are not listed as diphthongs in this text.

The Greek diphthongs can also be placed in the vowel rectangle, showing how they "cross the line" in moving from one position to another (see fig. 6).

The Pronunciation of New Testament Greek

The fact that certain diphthongs became *monophthongs* in the history of Greek creates a problem—that of the pronunciation of New Testament Greek. The pronunciation commonly used in American colleges and seminaries is an attempt to approximate that used by the Athenians during the classical period in Greece (fifth and fourth centuries B.C.). The pronunciation now used in modern Greece differs greatly from this and is much more difficult for English-speaking students. In general, the Greek of the classical period was a phonetic language—that is, its letters represented the sounds, and no heard sound was unexpressed in writing. In the course of history, however, many words retained their old spellings though their pronunciation had changed. How, then, was Greek pronounced in New Testament times?

Pronunciation of vowels

First, in classical Greek a long vowel took twice as long to pronounce as a short one. For example, o was distinguished from ω on the basis of quantity (length) as well as quality (articulation). Quantitative distinction was lost in Greek before the time of Christ, and is not maintained in the standard academic pronunciation. Second, in New Testament times there was a tendency to give the pronunciation of iota to a number of other vowels and diphthongs, such as η, υ, ει, and οι. This drift toward the iota sound is called *itacism*. Itacism accounts for several common types of scribal error in New Testament manuscripts, such as the substitution of vowels in the Greek personal pronouns (as ἡμεῖς / ὑμεῖς, ἡμῖν / ὑμῖν, and ἡμᾶς / ὑμᾶς). The final tendency concerning vowels has already been noted: the gradual replacement of diphthongs with monophthongs, blotting out, for example, the difference between ει and η.

Pronunciation of consonants

During the New Testament period, most of the Greek consonants were pronounced as in figure 4 (see p. 35). The sibilant σ was always voiceless (as in *hiss*), though the voiced sound (as in *his*) was heard before voiced consonants, as in σβέννυμι, "I quench." The z sound in ζ gradually silenced the d sound, until in the koine period ζ was equivalent to the English z (as in *zeal*). Also during this period the letter ρ was probably trilled, as it is today in many European languages.

Changes involving the aspirates were far-reaching. The three letters φ, θ, and χ were at one time equivalent to the three voiceless stops π, τ, and κ plus the sound of the rough breathing (*aspiration*). They were more or less pronounced as follows: φ like *ph* in flop-*h*ouse; θ like *th* in pot-*h*ead; and χ like *kh* in block-*h*ead. English, too, makes a distinction between aspirated and unaspirated p, t, and k sounds. If you hold your hand in front of your mouth when saying *pin*, you will feel the aspiration—a short blast of air. Then try *spin*, and you will find that p in this position is much less heavily aspirated. The same is true of the t and k sounds, as in *top* and *stop*, *cat* and *scat*. English does not make a distinction in spelling between the variant sounds of *p*, *t*, and *k*, but Greek did. Knowing that φ, θ, and χ were once pronounced π‧, τ‧, and κ‧ will be helpful in recognizing changes in the spelling of certain words involving aspirates.

Phonemics: Sounds as System

As we have already indicated, phonology is concerned not only with sounds but with sound systems. We have already attempted to describe, as briefly and succinctly as possible, the characteristics of the "raw materials" of the Greek language, the speech sounds out of which the language is made. Taken independently these sound units are meaningless, but when they combine into larger units they become carriers of meaning—a fact which is at the heart of phonemics.

Phonemes

Languages are made up of organized sounds. All the other units of language—morphemes, words, sentences, paragraphs, discourses—are ultimately composed of different combinations and recombinations of these sounds. The technical name for these units, as we have seen, is phoneme. A phoneme is a sound that the native speaker of a language knows to be a meaningful part of that language and that enables him to make distinctions between words, in contrast to a *phone*, which is any simple, objective language sound as it would be recorded by an instrument in the laboratory. The native speaker of English can distinguish between *bill* and *fill* because of the difference between *b* and *f*. The same difference allows the speaker of Greek to distinguish between βαίνω ("I go") and φαίνω ("I shine"). Likewise, in Greek κ and χ are different phonemes because they affect meaning: ἐκει means "there," and ἐχει means "he has." Even the smallest phonemic change can have a strong impact on meaning. In John 20:31, for example, the manuscripts are divided between πιστεύητε ("that you keep believing"), implying that the gospel is for those who are already believers, and πιστεύσητε ("that you may believe"), implying that it is addressed to non-Christians. Similarly, in Romans 5:1 one phoneme makes the difference between *"we have* peace with God" (ἔχομεν) or *"let us have* peace with God" (ἔχωμεν).

Allophones

In addition to phonemes like *b* and *f*, there are variants, or *allophones* (Gk. ἄλλος, 'other' + φωνή, 'sound'), of the same phoneme. For example, notice again the difference between the way you pronounce the *p* in *pin* and the *p* in *spin*. The *p* in *pin* is pronounced with a slight puff of air after it, whereas the *p* in *spin* is not. The sort of difference exhibited by the two English *p* sounds is called a *phonetic* (meaningless) one as contrasted with a *phonemic* (meaningful) one. That is, aspirated *p* in English (as in *pin*) does not affect the meaning of a word, since to a native speaker of the language it sounds the same as unaspirated *p*. In Greek, however, aspirated π' (spelled φ) *did* affect meaning, and so was considered a different phoneme. This distinction between phonemes and allophones allows us to recognize two levels of phonological representation— the level of pronunciation or what can be called the phonetic level, and the level of contrast or opposition, the phonemic level.

An obvious example of a Greek allophone is nasal-γ. Nasal-γ is actually not a separate phoneme in Greek since it merely takes the place of ν before the velars κ, γ, χ, and ξ, as in ἄγκυρα, "anchor." In other words, nasal-γ is an *allophone* of ν before velars. The *ng* sound represented by γ even had a special name in Greek, ἄγμα, but this term has never been adopted by the authors of Greek grammars.

Suprasegmental Features

In addition to phonemes and allophones, there are linguistic features that are not necessarily restricted to a single sound segment but may apply to several segments at one time. These features are referred to as *suprasegmental features*, and they include such things as *stress* (cf. the noun *permit* with the verb *permit*), *pitch* (cf. "What's on the road ahead?" with "What's on the road, a head?"), and *juncture* (cf. *nitrate* with *night rate*). Suprasegmental features might seem to be unimportant to students of the written New Testament, but the sound of Greek can play an important role in several areas, including the science of textual criticism. For example, juncture can help explain the variant in 1 Thessalonians 2:7, where the pronunciation of ἐγενήθημεν ἤπιοι ("we became gentle") would be almost indistinguishable from ἐγενήθημεν νήπιοι ("we became babes"), and vice versa.

The phonologist has only begun his work when he has isolated the phonemes, allophones, and suprasegmental features of a language. He must go on to provide as complete a discussion as possible of the entire sound system of the language with which he is working. Part of this task is to discover the order underlying what seems on the surface to be irregularity. Linguists know that speech is governed by an orderly system of rules. When this system is obscured by surface appearances the phonologist uses his linguistic knowledge to explain the situation. He may show that what seems to be an "irregular" form is not irregular at all, but is in fact quite predictable in terms of the phonological rules of the language. For example, he may demonstrate that what appears to be a chaotic and senseless spelling—such as ἔχω becoming ἕξω (with rough breathing) in the future tense—is actually a sensible spelling in terms of the underlying structure.

This is not to say that the phonologist will always be able to explain every seeming irregularity. No one, not even a phonologist, could make the Greek verb ἐσθίω regular, given the aorist form ἔφαγον. But in many cases the phonologist can show that underlying the surface chaos is an orderly system that, once understood, will make the correct identification of forms a matter of course rather than of guessing.

Common Phonological Processes in Greek

Because of the irregularities alluded to above, one of the major aims of phonology is the discovery and explanation of phonological processes. The term *phonological process*, as it is used here, refers to any systematic sound change that affects a class of sounds (such as fricatives or velars) or a sound sequence (such as a series of aspirated consonants). Linguists who are concerned with phonological processes necessarily assume that there is a basic or underlying form, which is called the *phonological representation*. This form is modified by a process, resulting in a new or changed form. If this is the actual spoken form, it is called the *surface form* or the *phonetic representation*.

To illustrate just one type of phonological process, linguists often discuss the process of *cluster reduction* that is exhibited by young children. Typically, one element of a cluster is deleted, usually the more "difficult" one, resulting in a simplified phonetic structure. When initial *s* comes before a stop such as *p*, the *s* is usually deleted by a process of "*s*-cluster reduction." So, for example, we find a two-year-old saying *poon* instead of *spoon*. The child's basic or underlying form is *spoon*, which is also the adult surface form. This underlying form is then modified by a phonological process, giving the child's surface form *poon*.

Languages undergo many such changes, and these changes frequently occur with some degree of regularity. Careful study of phonological change in Greek has led scholars to identify the following principles that occur with varying degrees of consistency.

Vowel Changes

Apophony

It is obvious that the words λέγω ("I speak") and λόγος ("word") are related. Yet why should the root vowel not show a regular correspondence (either λεγ or λογ)? The solution to this problem lies in the fact that Greek possesses a system of *apophony*. Apophony (also called *Ablaut* or *qualitative vowel gradation*) is the alteration of internal vowels of a root to effect change in meaning. In Arabic, for example, there is a root *slm*, which means "to be peaceful, safe, submissive." By inserting a short *a* after each of the letters, we get the form *salama*, "he was peaceful." If, on the other hand, we insert a short *a* after the *s* and a long *ā* after the *l*, the noun *salām*, "peace," is obtained. Yet another noun, *islām*, meaning "submission, reconciliation," can be formed by adding a short *i* before the *s* and a long *ā* after the *l*. Finally, if we prefix the participial marker *mu-* and add a long *ī* after the *l*, the participle *muslīm*, "one who submits," is the result.

Evidences of apophony are found in all Indo-European languages. In English we encounter the words *sing*, *sang*, and *sung*, in which the change in vowels indicates the tense of the verb. By giving still another vowel quality, that of *o*, we are even able to form a noun from the verb, namely *song*.

One of the most obvious cases of Greek apophony is found in the verbal system. Consider the following forms of the verb λείπω, "I leave":

Present	Aorist	Perfect
λείπω	ἔλιπον	λέλοιπα

Notice that in the present tense we have λειπ, in the aorist λιπ, and in the perfect λοιπ. Similarly we find πείθω, "I persuade," but πέποιθα, "I trust"; φεύγω, "I flee," but ἔφυγον, "I fled." (Prefixes and suffixes were also used, but these are not essential to our point here.) Another case of Greek apophony is the alternation of ε and ο to form nouns from verbs. Thus, φέρω, "I carry," becomes φόρος, "a burden"; τρέπω, "I turn," becomes τροπή, "a turning"; τείνω, "I stretch," becomes τόνος, "a stretch of the string, a tone"; and, as we saw above, λέγω, "I speak," becomes λόγος, "a word."

Quantitative vowel gradation

Of the seven vowels in Greek, ε and ο are always short, and their counterparts η and ω are always long. The vowels α, ι, and υ may be either long or short. *Quantitative vowel gradation* is a term used to describe the change in the quantity or length of the vowels in related word forms. We encounter this primarily in the future and aorist stems of *contract verbs*, that is, verbs with the stem ending in -αω, -οω, and -εω (e.g., τιμάω, but τιμήσω, ἐτίμησα; δηλόω, but δηλώσω, ἐδήλωσα) and in the inflection of certain nouns (e.g., γλῶσσα, γλώσσης; ἄρχων, ἄρχοντος). Sometimes the initial short vowel of a word forming the second part of a compound is lengthened, as in στρατηγός, "a general," from στρατός, "army," and ἄγω, "I lead."

A particular type of change related to quantitative vowel gradation is a process known as *compensatory lengthening*. This involves a word that contains a short vowel followed by two consonants, one of which is dropped. The vowel is then lengthened to "compensate" for the lost consonant. In this way the aorist indicative of μένω ("I remain"), ἔμεινα, is formed from ἐμενσα; the σ has dropped out of the word and the preceding vowel has been lengthened. The resulting diphthong is called "spurious" because it was formed by compensatory lengthening and would not otherwise have occurred. Note that the rules for lengthening are slightly different from those involved in *augmentation* (e.g., ε becomes ει, not η; ο becomes ου, not ω).

Addition of vowels

Occasionally a short vowel is placed before a consonant at the beginning of a word, especially when there is an initial cluster of consonants. This process, known as *prothesis* (Gk. πρό, 'before' + τίθημι, 'I place'), is common in Spanish: Latin *schola*, "school," is *escuela* in Spanish, while Latin *status*, "state," corresponds to *estado* in Spanish. Because initial *s* plus a stop cluster is not allowed in Spanish, native Spanish speakers frequently add the prothetic vowel *e* to such words as *school* and *store* when speaking English. Examples of prothesis in Greek include ἀ-λείφω, "I anoint with oil" (from λίπος, 'fat'); ἐ-χθές, "yesterday"; ἐ-μός, "my"; ἐ-κεῖ, "there"; and ἐ-θέλω, "I wish."

Epenthesis (Gk. ἐπεν, 'up in' + τίθημι, 'I place' = 'I insert') is the insertion of an extra sound within a word. English speakers often insert an epenthetic vowel in words such as *athlete* ("athalete") and *elm* ("elem"), and children may insert an *e* after the *b* in *blue* or after the *g* in *green*. In Greek, epenthesis occurs in words like βαίνω, "I go," and αἴρω, "I raise," where the ι has been inserted into the root of each word.

Loss of vowels

Loss of vowels (and therefore syllables) is especially common in languages that place strong stress upon one syllable of a word. As a result of the emphasis on the stressed syllable, other syllables in the word tend to become reduced, slurred, or even lost. When the lost vowel is at the end of the word, the loss is termed *apocope* (Gk. ἀποκοπή, 'a cutting off'); when a medial vowel drops, the process is called *syncope* (Gk. συγκοπή, 'a cutting up').

Syncope is a common phonological process in English. Words such as *family*, *frightening*, and *interest* often are pronounced without the post-tonic vowel (the one following the stressed vowel). Greek, too, provides numerous examples of syncope. We can see it reflected in the spelling of πατρός (for πατερός). This word was stressed on the final syllable, and by the classical period people had begun to slur the preceding vowel, and the medial vowel eventually disappeared. Likewise we find πίπτω for πι-πετ-ω, and γίγνομαι (Koine γίνομαι) for γι-γεν-ομαι.

Apocope is rare in Greek. In literature apocope is confined to poetry. In Homer we find ἄν, κάτ, and πάρ for ἀνά, κατά, and παρά. Apocope occurs rarely in Attic poetry and never in New Testament Greek.

Euphony of vowels

The Greek ear did not like the immediate succession of vowels. Many changes, therefore, were made for the sake of *euphony* (Gk. εὖ, 'good' + φωνή, 'sound'). To avoid having to make a slight pause between vowels to allow each to be sounded separately, various devices were employed: *contraction*, the fusion of two vowels (or a vowel and a diphthong) within a word; *elision*, the omission of a short final vowel before another word beginning with a vowel; *crasis*, the contraction of final and initial vowels of words, thus joining two words into one; and *movable consonants*, added to the end of words when the next word began with a vowel.

Contraction brings words together according to regular patterns. These patterns may be reduced to a relatively few principles. For example, two vowels that may naturally form a diphthong do so, so that α + ι = αι; ο + ι = οι; and ε + υ = ευ. Other rules governing contraction, simplified for easy memorization, can be found in most Greek grammars.

Elision (Lat. *elido*, 'I strike out'), the omission of a short final vowel before an initial vowel, is marked with an apostrophe ('). Common New Testament examples are δι' αὐτοῦ (for διὰ αὐτοῦ, see John 1:3) and ἀλλ' ἵνα (for ἀλλὰ ἵνα, see John 1:8). Elision occurs frequently with adverbs, prepositions, and conjunctions, but does not affect certain prepositions (such as πρό and περί), the conjunction ὅτι, and the forms that regularly take movable ν.

Crasis (Gk. κρᾶσις, 'a mingling') is the contraction of the final and initial vowels of successive words so that the two words are written as one. The mark used to indicate such contraction is called a *coronis* ('). There are similarities between crasis in Greek and English words like *aren't, can't, I'm,* and *you're.* The most common New Testament forms are τοὔνομα (τὸ ὄνομα), ταὐτά (τὰ αὐτά), κἀγώ (καὶ ἐγώ), κἀμοί (καὶ ἐμοί), and κἀκεῖ (καὶ ἐκεῖ).

Finally, the movable consonant ν, added to the end of a word when the following word begins with a vowel, is regularly found in words ending in -σι, -ξι, or -ψι, to the third person singular verb forms ending in -ε, and to ἐστί. However, in New Testament Greek ν was sometimes added indiscriminately to forms other than those listed above. Some scholars call this usage "irrational ν." Movable ς is added to a few New Testament words, such as οὕτως, ἄχρις, and μέχρις, for the same reason as movable ν—to avoid the succession of vowels between words.

Consonant Changes

Assimilation of consonants

Perhaps the most common type of conditioned sound change

involving consonants is *assimilation* (Lat. *assimilo*, 'I make similar'), whereby one sound becomes more like a neighboring one. Assimilation occurs frequently in practically every language. It can be considered a simplification of the muscular movements needed to pronounce a given word. In terms of articulation, assimilation of consonants usually involves one consonant becoming more like another in point of articulation, manner of articulation, and/or voicing. Assimilations are also divided into two broad groups depending on the direction of the change. *Regressive assimilation* means that a consonant becomes more like the one that follows; in other words, the force of the change proceeds backwards. *Progressive assimilation* takes place when the first consonant in some way makes the second more like itself.

By far, the most common type of assimilation is regressive. An English example is the word *imperfect*, which contains a root, *perfect*, and a prefix whose base form is *in-*. The change of *n*, an alveolar nasal continuant, to *m*, a bilabial nasal continuant, makes it more similar to the *p* in *perfect*, which is a bilabial stop. The assimilation of *n* is said to be conditioned by *p*—that is, the *n* shifts its point of contact to match that of *p*. Likewise in Greek, a preceding consonant is generally assimilated to a following consonant, as in ἐμμένω, "I abide by," for ἐν-μένω. In this case the alveolar nasal continuant ν has shifted its point of contact to match that of μ, a bilabial nasal continuant. If assimilation is complete—as with ἐμμένω—one sound takes on all the features of (and becomes identical to) another sound. If assimilation is partial—as with ἐπέμφθην, "I was sent," for ἐπέμπ-θην—one sound becomes more like another, taking on only some of its features.

Much less common than regressive assimilation is progressive assimilation, in which a consonant assumes some of the qualities of the one that precedes it. A historic English example is the Old English cluster *-ln-* becoming Middle English *-ll-* (as in Middle English *mille* ["mill"] from Old English *myln* [cf. Lat. *molinus*, 'of a mill']). A Greek example is the verb ὄλλυμι, "I destroy," for ὀλ-νυμι.

Dissimilation of consonants

In *dissimilation*, like assimilation, one sound has an effect on another, but in contrast to assimilation, the two sounds become less similar. An English example is *colonel*, in which the unstressed *l* was dissimilated to the *r* sound to avoid repetition. In Greek, λ sometimes becomes ρ, as in ἀργαλέος, "painful," for ἀλγαλεος (cf. ἄλγος, 'pain'). Otherwise, the process of dissimilation is rare in Greek.

Metathesis

A relatively uncommon type of sound change, though frequent enough to be worthy of mention, involves the reversing of position of two adjoining sounds, which is called *metathesis* (Gk. μετατίθημι, 'I transpose'). The person who says *tradegy* for *tragedy* or *revelant* for *relevant* is metathesizing. The dialect form *axe* for *ask* is another example, going back a thousand years to Old English. Greek examples of metathesis include Πνύξ, "the Pnyx," which in the genitive case appears as Πυκνός, and τίκτω, "I give birth," for τι-τκω (root τεκ, as in τέκνον, 'child').

Loss of consonants

The loss of a consonant in Greek can occur in several ways. In the first place, the only consonants that may stand at the end of a word in Greek are ν, ρ, and σ (ξ, ψ). As a result, in inflection it is sometimes necessary to drop a "not-permitted-as-final" consonant. Thus the word στόμα, "mouth," is from στοματ-, the formation involving the dropping of the final τ. The only exceptions to this rule are the preposition ἐκ, the negative adverb οὐκ, and foreign words taken over into Greek, such as Ἰσραήλ, Ἀβραάμ, and Δαυίδ.

Second, loss of σ is commonplace in Greek. Between vowels, σ is dropped. The loss of this so-called *intervocalic sigma* is seen both in verbs (λύη, "you loose yourself," for λυεσαι) and nouns (γένους, "of a race," for γενεσ-ος). Moreover, in the aorist of verbs whose stems end in λ, μ, ν, or ρ (the *liquid verbs*), σ usually disappears, with compensatory lengthening of the preceding vowel, as in ἔμεινα, "I remained," for ἐμεν-σα, and ἔστειλα, "I sent," for ἐστελ-σα. Further, initial σ before a vowel becomes the rough breathing. Examples include ἑπτά, "seven" (Lat. *septem*); ἥμισυς, "half" (Lat. *semi-*); and ἵστημι, "I place," for σι-στημι (cf. Lat. *sisto*).

Third, ϝ (digamma), an obsolete Greek letter, occasionally leaves traces. ϝ is called *digamma* because of its shape (it looks like two capital gammas on top of each other) or *waw* because of its pronunciation (it was pronounced like the English *w* or the Latin *v*). The following special cases are to be noted:

κλη(ϝ)ίς = Latin *clavis*, "key" (cf. Eng. *clavicord*).
(ϝ)ἔσπερος = Latin *vesper*, "evening" (cf. Eng. *vespers*).
(ϝ)ἴς = Latin *vis*, "vigor, might" (cf. Eng. *vim*).
(ϝ)ἰδεῖν = Latin *video*, "I see" (cf. Eng. *video*).
(ϝ)οἶνος = Latin *vinus*, "wine" (cf. Eng. *vine, wine*).
(ϝ) ἔργον = English *work* (cf. Ger. *Werk, work*).

Amalgamation

Changes in a consonant are sometimes brought about when a word inflects (i.e., as a word changes its form in the course of the declension of a noun or the conjugation of a verb), especially if it is brought together with another consonant. In this case, *amalgamation* is said to occur. For example, π, β, and φ amalgamate with a following σ to form the double consonant ψ, as in θλίβω, "I press," aorist ἔθλιψα. Before σ, the phonemes κ, γ, and χ amalgamate with the σ to form the double consonant ξ, as in ἄρχω, "I rule," future ἄρξω. Finally τ, δ, and θ may amalgamate with a following rough breathing to form θ, as in μετά + ἵστημι = μεθίστημι, "I transfer." Before σ, however, these same phonemes disappear, as in σπεύδω, "I hasten," future σπεύσω. Thus in the case of τ, δ, and θ followed by σ, the amalgamation effectively amounts to annihilation!

Deaspiration

The rough breathing, as an *aspirate* (*h*-sound), often disappears when the following syllable contains an aspirated consonant (φ, θ, or χ). This process of *deaspiration* is known today as "Grassman's Law" (see chapter 6). For example, the nominative θρίξ ("hair") becomes τριχός in the genitive case lest the word contain two successive aspirated consonants (θριχος). Thus the stem is τριχ in all forms of the inflection except where the χ amalgamates with σ to become ξ. This means that the form θρίξ is perfectly in accord with regular phonological rules, and is not actually irregular (though it certainly looks that way!). (Incidentally, from the nominative θρίξ and the genitive τριχός we get the zoological names *Ophiothrix* and *Trichina*.) Another example is the present tense verb form ἔχω, "I have," which stands for ἔχω (originally σεχω!). Here the rough breathing has changed to the smooth breathing before the aspirated consonant χ. The rough breathing reappears, however, in the future tense form ἕξω since the letter ξ allows the word to retain its original initial aspiration. Other examples of Greek deaspiration include πέφευγα, "I have fled," for φε-φευγα, and τίθημι, "I place," for θι-θημι. Deaspiration is not an invariable, however, and examples can be found where two aspirates occur at the beginning of successive syllables (e.g., the aorist passive form ἐξεχύθη, from ἐκχέω, "I pour out," appears in Acts 1:18).

Consonant change before ι

Numerous changes occur before the semivowel ι. These changes are relevant especially to the formation of the present tense stem of certain verbs. The combination of ι with a preceding consonant produces the following phonetic changes:

1. κι and χι become σσ (Attic Gk. ττ), as in φυλάσσω, "I guard," for φυλακιω (cf. φυλακή, "a guard"), and ταράσσω, "I disturb," for ταραχιω (cf. ταραχή, "disorder").
2. λι becomes λλ, as in ἄλλος, for ἀλιος (cf. Lat. *alius*, 'other').
3. τ before final ι often becomes σ, as in τίθησι, "he places," for τιθητι.
4. δι between vowels and γι after a vowel form ζ. Thus ἐλπίζω, "I hope," for ἐλπιδιω, and ἁρπάζω, "I seize," for ἁρπαγιω.

Such, in brief, are the main phonological processes in New Testament Greek. What were the causes for these changes? No one knows for sure, but every conceivable factor has been suggested to account for them, including race, climate, topography, diet, occupation, or the fact that some speakers were just too lazy to pronounce words clearly. The neogrammarians held that sound change is independent of semantic features and is merely a matter of articulatory habits. Others felt that some forms have more "semantic weight" than others, and that only weaker semantic forms tend to undergo sound change. Probably each view contains part of the explanation. Yet it must be remembered that the "rules" of phonetic change mentioned above are merely statements of what *did* occur, without any connotation of what *should have* occurred. In the final analysis, it does not matter whether an explanation can be given or not, for any such explanation is nothing more than a description of an observed phenomenon.

Why Study Phonology?

At this point the reader would be quite justified in feeling a bit overwhelmed by the subject of this chapter. The question of why the entire complicated phonological structure of Greek should be studied is a highly valid one. If, for example, we can now say, "β is a voiced bilabial stop," what have we really gained? Perhaps a measure of accuracy after, "Greek is a nice-sounding language." But have we really learned anything important about the Greek language that can make us better students of the New Testament?

Whatever else can be said about the importance of phonology, one fact seems to stand out: for even the most rudimentary understanding of a language we need to know the sounds of that language. Every verbal reference we make about Greek will involve the speech-producing organs, the vocal tract. Even when we are not verbalizing Greek a knowledge of the sounds of Greek and how they influence each other will immensely facilitate our ability to learn the forms of words, since variations in form are often due to phonological rules operating in the language. This chapter may also have some useful carry-overs to the study of rhythm and cadence and perhaps to the poetic and rhetorical analysis of such New Testament hymns as Philippians 2:6–11. An overview of the phonology of Greek might even free us from the universal fear of irregular verbs as we become devoted to the task of ferreting out for ourselves the principles upon which Greek spelling is based.

The approach to Greek phonology presented in this chapter will not only help us come to grips with the sounds of the language but possibly even to understand a more important point: that it is quite possible for even the beginning student to learn to listen to language and to build his own system of phonemic classification. The study of Greek phonology becomes a significant step for the student who realizes that it is less a switch in subject matter than it is in method. It is not a switch from unscientific terms to scientific ones as much as from giving answers to asking questions. The traditional student simply memorizes the principal parts of irregular verbs. The linguistics student prefers to analyze irregular forms, breaking them down into parts (phonemes) and exploring various solutions until he reaches a satisfactory conclusion. By approaching the Greek language with the same objectivity with which linguists have approached their investigations, he learns to substitute science for dogma and understanding for rote.

But phonology is not an end in itself. Though an important part of the Greek grammatical system, it is ancillary to the real purpose of language—that of communication. Teachers and students who merely adopt linguistic jargon like "monophthongization" are neither modern nor progressive. Only when linguistic analysis leads to a significant understanding of language in general can the process be justified. The ultimate purpose of phonology, therefore, is to get us to go beyond the sounds of Greek and look at the meaning those sounds are intended to convey. To examine this aspect of meaning we must now proceed to the next level of linguistic structure, the level of language forms.

Suggestions for Further Reading

There are very few general studies of Greek phonology available. Among those using a system of description similar to that adopted in this chapter are:

Funk, Robert W. *A Beginning-Intermediate Grammar of Hellenistic Greek*, 1:31–53; 3:1–22. Missoula, Mont.: Scholars Press, 1973.

LaSor, William Sanford. *Handbook of New Testament Greek, An Inductive Approach Based on the Greek Text of Acts*, 2:9–50. Grand Rapids: Eerdmans, 1973.

Smyth, Herbert W. *Greek Grammar*. Cambridge: Harvard University Press, 1920.

The student interested in a more advanced study of phonology should consult:

Jones, D. *The Phoneme: Its Nature and Use*. Cambridge, England: Heffer, 1950.

Pike, Kenneth L. *Phonetics: A Critical Analysis of Phonetic Theory and a Technic for the Practical Description of Sounds*. Ann Arbor: University of Michigan Press, 1943.

3

Morphology: The Anatomy of Greek Words

The Concept of the Morpheme

The phonological system of a language is concerned with the organization of sounds into basic units called phonemes (see chapter 2). These units are not significant in and of themselves, except to the extent that they serve to differentiate the meaning of words, as in *pill* versus *bill*. Phonemes do, however, fall into a distinctive pattern, since each language has its own organization of sounds.

Although the sounds of language are fascinating, they are primarily tools for the communication of meaning. Hence phonemes are combined into larger units that have recognizable meaning. These units are called morphemes, and the branch of linguistics dealing with these units of meaning is generally referred to as morphology.

The Morpheme Defined

The exact definition of a morpheme will differ from textbook to textbook, but all linguists generally consider morphemes the minimum units of speech conveying a specific meaning (concept) in a language. In chapter 1 we indicated that the English phonemic sequence *dog* has meaning. Because it cannot be divided into two or more meaningful units, it is classified as a morpheme. It is a *free morpheme* because it can form a word without being attached to any other form. The plural marker *-s* was also shown to have meaning and to be indivisible; hence it is also a morpheme. But because it can only be used when attached to another form, it is a *bound morpheme*. Thus *dog* is a word of one morpheme, *dogs* is a word of two.

Any linguistic form, then, that cannot be broken down into smaller meaningful units is a morpheme. A morpheme may consist of no more than one sound, such as *s*, or of many sounds, such as *Mississippi*. Care must be taken not to conclude that phonemically identical morphemes are the same until their meanings are known. For example, the word *hits* consists of the morphemes *hit* and *s*. But examine the following utterances:

> The car *hits* the mailbox.
> The singer had many *hits*.

In the above sentences, the phoneme *s* forms two different morphemes, meaning "third person singular" and "plural," respectively. Likewise, the *er* in *hitter* and *greater* forms two different morphemes, meaning "one who" and "comparative form of the adjective," respectively. Beginners in linguistics must be careful not to confuse such *homophones*—morphemes that are alike phonemically but different in meaning.

It is also important to remember that a given sound or sound sequence that functions as a morpheme in certain words is not necessarily a morpheme wherever it shows up. The *-s* in *thesis* is not a morpheme, nor is the *-er* in *cheer*. Because of these sources of possible confusion, all definitions in morphemic analysis are considered tentative, final definition being left to context and usage.

Roots and Affixes

Morphemes may also be classified according to the way in which they function in a word. Those morphemes that form the nucleus of a word are *roots* or *bases*, while morphemes added to these roots are *affixes*. In *talks, talked,* and *talking, talk* is the root and *-s, -ed,* and *-ing* are affixes. Affixes added to the ends of roots, as in the examples given, are *suffixes*, whereas those placed before the root, as *un-* and *re-* in *untie* and *retie*, are *prefixes*. Affixes appearing in the middle of morphemes are *infixes*. Infixes are found commonly in only a few languages, notably Hebrew and Arabic.

A root must be carefully distinguished from a *stem*. A stem is any construction to which an affix can be added. Whereas roots always contain a single morpheme, a stem may consist of a root plus an affix. For example, *dress* is a single morpheme. In the verb *undress*, *dress* is the root to which *un-* is prefixed. It is also the stem. In *undressing*, *dress* is still the root or base, but *undress* is the stem with the suffix *-ing*. Thus, all roots are stems, but not all stems are roots. In the word *blackbirds*, *black* and *bird* are roots, while *blackbird* is the stem to which the suffix *-s* is attached. Stems that consist of two roots are called *compounds*.

Hypothetically there is no limit to the potential combination of morphemes in a single word. A magnificent example of how a word can be created by the combination of prefixes and suffixes is *antidisestablishmentarianism*—the longest word in English outside of technical scientific terminology. This monstrosity has a root of three letters (*sta*), with three prefixes (*anti-*, *dis-*, and *e-* [from *ex*]), and six suffixes (*-bl* [from *able*], *-ish*, *-ment*, *-ari*, *-an*, and *-ism*). It means "the theory in opposition to the idea that the church should be separated from the state." *Sta*, the root, means "to stand" (cf. Gk. ἵστημι, 'I stand,' root στα). *Stable* is an adjective meaning "able to stand" ("sta-able"). To *establish* means "to make able to stand alone." Here the *e-* (from Lat. *ex*) means "apart," and *-ish* means "to make." *Establishment*, therefore, is "the act or result of making to stand alone," while *disestablishment* is the undoing of all this; it is the active negation, the opposite, just as "disease" is the opposite of "ease" or "comfort." The suffix *-ari* (*ary* when final) means "in the nature of," and *-an*, "one who." Thus a *disestablishmentarian* is "one who favors the undoing of the act of making something [here the church] able to stand alone." Now add *anti-* ("against") and *-ism* ("theory or belief") and we have it all: "The theory (*ism*) of those who (*arian*) oppose (*anti*) the breakdown (*dis*) of the organization of church and state (*establishment*)."

Derivational and Inflectional Affixes

We have seen that morphemes can be classified as either free or bound, roots or affixes. Root morphemes carry the central core of the meaning of the word, whereas affixes are added to roots to give additional form or meaning. However, not all affixes are alike in the effects they have on the roots or stems to which they are affixed. Generally speaking, affixes fall into two major classifications. *Derivational affixes* either indicate word class (cf. *common* [adj.] and *commonly* [adv.]) or else add lexical meaning (e.g., *un-* in *uncommon*). *Inflectional affixes* serve as signaling devices to show such grammatical characteristics as person (*I sing* vs. *he sings*), number (*hat* vs. *hats*), tense (*dream* vs. *dreamed*), case (*girl* vs. *girl's*), and comparison (*nice* vs. *nicer* vs. *nicest*). In other words, an inflectional affix has the function of distinguishing various forms of the same word, whereas a derivational affix forms a part of the root to which it is attached. When an affix of this latter type occurs with a word, it occurs in all forms of it and thus forms a new word rather than just another grammatical form of the old word. This distinction between derivational and inflectional affixes must constantly be kept in mind when reading Greek.

Allomorphs

Just as variant forms of phonemes are called allophones, some morphemes have variant forms known as *allomorphs* (Gk. ἄλλος, 'another' + μορφή, 'form'). Allomorphs are variations in the phonological shape of a morpheme. Consider, for example, the verb form *hits* in the sentence *The player hits the ball*. The final *s* represents the third person singular present tense morpheme in English. If you now replace *hits* with *holds*, you will notice that this same verb ending is pronounced differently. This is because the final *s* is voiced in English after a voiced stop like *d* but voiceless after a voiceless stop like *t*. In other words, the same morpheme may appear in different phonetic shapes, depending upon the language situation (environment) in which it is found. Similarly, the past tense morpheme, represented by *-d* and *-ed* in *deceived* and *walked*, has two phonetic representations that are predictable on the basis of the preceding sound. In Greek, ἐκ and ἐξ are allomorphs because they have identical meaning and differ only in regard to the language situation (ἐκ before consonants, ἐξ before vowels). Many other Greek prepositions have allomorphs. For example, ἀπό, ἀπ᾽, and ἀφ᾽ are simply allomorphs of the same morpheme.

However, in word pairs such as *man/men, child/children, sheep/sheep*, in which the second item can be said to contain the plural allomorph, we cannot state the variation between the two forms solely in terms of phonetic environment. Instead, we must refer to the morphemes *man, child,* and *sheep,* and then specify the allomorph of the plural morpheme separately for each. This kind of variation among allomorphs is called *morphological conditioning*. The morphologically conditioned allomorphs of a morpheme are regarded as irregular in contrast with the *phonologically conditioned* allomorphs (such as the plural marker in *hits* and *holds*) that are regarded as regular. *Men, children,* and *sheep* are therefore irregular English plural allomorphs, just as *drank, swam,* and *was* are irregular past tense allomorphs of *drink, swim,* and *am.*

Morphemes and Words

Obviously much of what has been said about morphemes is a way to discuss linguistically the make-up of what are normally referred to as "words." The *word* has yet to be given a satisfactory universal definition. People sometimes assume that a word is recognizable because it represents a "whole thought" or a "complete thing." But this view is clearly wrong when one looks at the lack of correspondence between words from different languages. In English, the four words *train operator's educational license* correspond to one in German, *Lokomotivführerausbildungsbescheinigung.* Or the six words *He used to teach in Athens* are translated by two in Greek, Ἀθήναις ἐδίδασκεν.

Perhaps the best-known definition is that proposed by the American linguist Leonard Bloomfield, who defined a word as a minimal free form, that is, the smallest form that can occur by itself. Such a definition works fairly well for written English, but otherwise it is not very helpful.

First, linguists are concerned with the spoken word as well as the written word, and the two do not necessarily coincide. For example, in conversational Spanish you might hear a sentence that sounded like a single word:

Estosombresondecuador.

Actually, a native Spanish speaker would be able to identify five words in the sentence, which is written as:

Estos hombres son de Ecuador.
(These men are from Ecuador.)

That the Spanish speaker recognizes these words is certainly not because of any pauses between them. Second, there are a number of writing systems that do not leave spaces between words (in fact, ancient Greek often joined all the words together). Third, even in English we cannot determine in every case whether or not something is a word just by following Bloomfield's definition. Is *matchbox* a word, but not *match box* or *match-box,* each of which is generally considered to be correct?

To complicate matters even more, a single sequence of phonemes such as *h-i-t* can represent a *phonological word*, more than one
lexical item (the technical term for "dictionary entry"), and more
than one *syntactic word* (i.e., a word combined with other words in a
sentence):

Phonological Word	*Lexical Items*	*Syntactic Words*
hit	*hit*: noun	*hit*: noun (The play was a *hit*)
	hit: verb	*hit*: present tense verb (The players *hit* the ball)
		hit: past tense verb (He *hit* me)
		hit: past participle (He was *hit* by the ball)

To be sure, this is an extreme example. Compared with many
languages, there are relatively few differences between the various
types of words in English. But in a highly inflected language like
Greek, a lexical item often has several different syntactic as well as
phonological forms. For instance, the lexical item λόγος has ten
different syntactic forms, and nine different phonological forms.
The endings vary systematically, depending on usage: λόγος is the
subject, λόγον the object. Therefore, the linguist's use of terms
such as *free* and *bound*, *root* and *affix*, and *inflectional* and *derivational* is
necessary for a complete, clear, and explicit description of the
"word."

We now turn our attention to the morphology of the words in
the New Testament. Because of the complexity of the Greek
morphological system, this chapter is perhaps the most technical
part of this volume. If the material presented here is new to you, I
suggest that you do not try to absorb every detail as you read, but
scan quickly over the entire chapter to get a broad view of the
subject. Then, as time and inclination permit, return for a more
detailed study of those areas that seem interesting and important.
As you read, keep in mind that there is no sharp dividing line
between phonology and morphology, just as there is no clear
demarcation between morphology and syntax.

The Greek Morphological System

Basic to understanding the structure of the Greek language is
being able to visualize the morphological system by means of

which its words and phrases are constructed. Since a word may be made up of several morphemes, we must have a procedure for identifying these minimal parts. The procedure used is a process of *substitution* and *comparison*. Two or more utterances partly alike but partly different are compared. The like parts, if they have similar meanings, constitute a *frame* in which the unlike parts substitute for one another. Comparing the words ἄδολος, ἄζυμος, ἄθεος, and ἀδύνατος with δόλος, ζύμος, θεός, and δύνατος, the morpheme ἀ can be isolated. This morpheme, plus an adjacent slot where the other stems can be substituted for one another, constitute a frame:

	ἀ		

When the stems in question are substituted for each other in the frame, it is found that there is an accompanying change in the total meaning of each of the four utterances:

		δολ	ος	= guile-less
	ἀ	ζυμ	ος	= leaven-less
		θε	ος	= God-less
		δυνατ	ος	= power-less

Comparisons and contrasts such as these make morpheme identification possible.

We have seen that a morpheme, either free or bound, that carries the basic meaning of a Greek word is called the root, to which one or more bound forms may be affixed. These affixes are of three kinds according to their position with respect to the root: prefixes are added before the root (as in ἀ-δύνατος); suffixes are attached to the end of the root (as in πνεῦ-μα); and infixes are inserted in the root (as in βαίνω, from the root βαν). Since Greek affixes are either derivational or inflectional in function, they can be discussed under these two categories.

The Derivational System

Derivational affixes in Greek may be either prefixes or suffixes. Prefixes like ἀ- (ἀνομία), ἀμφι- (ἀμφιβάλλω), εὐ- (εὐαγγέλιον), and παν- (πάντοτε) serve to give words additional meaning. Conversely, derivational suffixes like -σις (κρίσις), -μος (σεισμός), -της (μαθητής), and -ως (ἀληθῶς) determine the word class (part of speech) of a particular language form. They may also add lexical meaning. Thus, καλός ("good") is an adjective, but καλῶς ("well") is an adverb; γραφή ("a writing") is a noun, but γράφω ("I write") is a verb; κρίσις ("judgment") denotes the act of judging, while κρίμα ("punishment") indicates the resulting sentence; and so forth. Greek makes a great deal of use of derivational affixes to make new words from existing roots.

Word formation takes place frequently in all languages, but it occurs more frequently in Greek than in English. You will find it one of the most practical areas of study in building a Greek vocabulary. Just as knowing what basic English morphemes mean helps you to understand the difference between *friend, friendship, friendliness,* and *unfriendly,* so also knowing the significance of Greek derivational morphemes can aid you in the knowledge of Greek word meanings.

For example, from the root δικ ("to show, point out the thing that is right") over fifteen Greek words are formed, including:

δίκη	justice, right
δικάζω	I render justice, judge
δικαστής	a judge
δικασμός	a giving of justice
δικάσιμος	judicial
δίκαιος	just, righteous
δικαιόω	I declare righteous
δικαιοσύνη	righteousness
δικαίως	justly

Merely by adding the so-called *alpha-privative* (see p. 63) to the root, the following negative words are formed:

ἀδικέω	I am unjust, do wrong
ἀδίκημα	an injustice, a crime
ἀδικία	injustice, unrighteousness
ἀδικοκρίτης	an unjust judge
ἄδικος	unjust, unrighteous
ἀδίκως	unjustly

Add a preposition, and the following compound words result:

ἀντίδικος	enemy, opponent
ἐκδικέω	I punish, take vengeance for
ἐκδίκησις	punishment, vengeance
ἔκδικος	a punisher, avenger
ἔνδικος	just, deserved
καταδικάζω	I condemn
καταδίκη	condemnation

From the lengthened root δεικ the following words can be added to our list:

δείκνυμι	I show, point out
δεῖγμα	a thing shown, a pattern
δειγματίζω	I make a public show of
δειγματισμός	a public showing
δεικτήριον	a place for showing
δείκτης	an exhibitor
δεικτικός	able to show
δεῖξις	a showing, displaying

Now add a preposition to the longer root and the following compounds are formed:

ἀναδείκνυμι	I show clearly, appoint
ἀνάδειξις	a showing forth, commissioning
ἀποδείκνυμι	I show, prove, attest
ἀπόδειξις	a proof
ἐνδείκνυμι	I show, demonstrate
ἔνδειξις	a proof, sign
παραδειγματίζω	I hold up to contempt, expose
ὑπόδειγμα	example, model, pattern
ὑποδείκνυμι	I show, prove

The above examples relative to the δικ- root not only illustrate the importance of knowing the basic meanings of roots and stems, but also the importance of knowing the significance of the morphemes added to them. When the meaning of these morphemes is added to the meaning of the root or stem, a combined or modified meaning results. Thus ἀδίκημα ("an injustice") is related to δίκη ("justice") but it has a different meaning because of the morphemes added to the beginning (ἀ-) and the ending (-μα) of the root.

Prefixed derivational morphemes

Prefixed morphemes are capable of modifying the meanings of roots and stems in important ways. Greek has both free and bound derivational prefixes. *Free form prefixes* (also called *separable particles*) can occur alone as well as be attached to words. The adverb πάντοτε, for example, contains a free form prefix, πάν (the neuter form of πᾶς), that has meaning even when it is not attached to τότε. Both as it stands alone and when it is used in composition it means "all" or "every" (cf. *Pan-American, panorama, pantheist, panoply*). On the other hand, *bound form prefixes* (also called *inseparable particles*) cannot be used alone; they must be bound to a word. The prefix ἀμφι- ("around, on both sides") in ἀμφιβάλλω is a bound form because it is not used as a separate word, though it has meaning while it is attached to βάλλω ("I throw").

The New Testament contains several free form prefixes. The most common is εὐ-, which occurs in over one hundred different Greek words. The following list includes some of the more common words containing free form prefixes. (Words enclosed in brackets are English derivatives or words related in other ways to the Greek word.)

Prefix	Meaning	Example	Definition
εὐ-	good, well	εὐαγγέλιον	good news, gospel [evangel]
		εὐδοκία	good thinking, pleasure
		εὐλογία	praise, blessing [eulogy]
		εὐσεβεία	reverence, piety [Eusebius]
		εὐχαριστία	thanksgiving [Eucharist]
		εὐλογητός	blessed, praised
παν-	all, every	παντοκράτωρ	the Almighty
		πανταχοῦ	everywhere
		πάντοτε	always, at all times
		πάντως	by all means, certainly
ἀγαν-	very	ἀγανακτέω	I am vexed, grieved
ἀρτι-	lately	ἀρτιγέννητος	lately born
παλιν-	again	παλινγενεσία	new birth, regeneration
τηλε-	afar off	τηλαυγῶς	at a distance

Bound form prefixes have meaning only when affixed to words.

The most common bound form prefix in the New Testament is the alpha-privative, found in at least three hundred different words. It is formed from the adverb ἄνευ ("without"); it occurs as ἀ- before words beginning with a consonant (e.g., ἀδικία) and as ἀν- before words beginning with a vowel (e.g., ἀνυπόκριτος). Care should be taken to avoid confusing this use of ἀ- with the *alpha-copulative* or *alpha-intensive* (see below) as well as with several other prefixed morphemes that also begin with an alpha (ἀμφι-, ἀνα-, ἀντι-, ἀπο-, and ἀρχ-).

As a prefix, alpha-privative is used in a negative sense and can be expressed in English by the morphemes *un-, in-, non-,* and so forth. In addition to having this negative meaning, the alpha prefix can also indicate union and togetherness (alpha-copulative) or intensification (alpha-intensive). The alpha-copulative is related to the particle ἅμα ("together") and denotes unity, community, or equality. Only a few New Testament words contain an alpha-copulative, but those that do occur quite frequently (e.g., ἀδελφός, ἀκολουθέω). The alpha-intensive is related either to the preposition ἀνά ("up, again") or the adverb ἄγαν ("very") and intensifies the force of a word.

Prefix	Meaning	Example	Definition
ἀ-privative	not, without	ἀκαθαρσία	uncleanness
		ἀνομία	lawlessness
		ἀτιμία	dishonor
		ἄκαρπος	unfruitful
		ἀνυπόκριτος	without hypocrisy, genuine
		ἀτιμάζω	I dishonor, insult
ἀ-copulative	with, union	ἀδελφός	brother, from the same womb (δελφύς)
		ἅπας	all together, whole, every
		ἀκολουθέω	I follow along the same path (κέλευθος)
ἀ-intensive	very, much	ἀτενίζω	I gaze steadfastly
		ἀσέλγεια	excess, licentiousness
ἀμφι-		on both sides	ἀμφιβάλλω	I throw around, cast a net

		ἀμφίβληστρον	a casting-net
ἀρχι-	chief, first	ἀρχάγγελος	archangel
		ἀρχηγός	founder, one who leads (ἄγω) first
δυσ-	ill, difficult	δυσβάστακτος	difficult to carry
		δυσφημία	ill-speaking (φημί)
ἡμι-	half	ἡμιθανής	half-dead
		ἡμίωρον	half an hour
νη-	not, without	νηστεία	fasting, without eating (ἐσθίω)
		νηστεύω	I fast

Suffixed derivational morphemes

The suffix morpheme stands between a word's root and its declensional or conjugational ending. Suffixes often have special meanings, and when these are known it is possible to deduce the meaning of an unfamiliar Greek word by analyzing the root idea as qualified by the suffix.

There are too many derivational suffixes in the Greek language to include in an introductory text; only the more common ones are listed below. Once you know the declensions and conjugations of Greek nouns, adjectives, verbs, and adverbs, you will be able to recognize the formative suffix as it appears with various endings.

The following list enumerates some of the *noun suffixes*:

1. Nouns denoting *action* or *process* are formed with -σις (-τις, -μις, -ψις), -μος, -εια, and -μη.

Suffix	Example	Definition
-σις	ἀνάστασις	raising, resurrection
	ἀποκάλυψις	revealing, revelation [Apocalypse]
	βρῶσις	eating, corrosion
	θλίψις	pressing, tribulation
	κρίσις	judging, judgment [crisis]
	κτίσις	creating, creation
	παράδοσις	a handing down, tradition
	πίστις	faith, belief, trust
-μος	ἁγιασμός	setting apart, sanctification
	διαλογισμός	reasoning, debating [dialogue]
	θερισμός	harvesting, harvest time [thermal]
	ὀφθαλμός	seeing, eye [ophthamologist]

	πειρασμός	a trying, testing, tempting
	ποταμός	a flowing, river, stream [hippopotamus]
-εια	ἀπώλεια	destruction [Apollyon]
	βασιλεία	rule, reign, kingdom
	πορνεία	fornication, immorality [pornography]
	προφητεία	prophesying, prophecy
-μη	γνώμη	decision, opinion
	δοκιμή	testing, proving
	περιτομή	circumcision
	τιμή	honor, esteem

2. Nouns denoting *result* are formed with -μα and -ος.

Suffix	Example	Definition
-μα	γράμμα	letter, writing [grammar]
	κρίμα	judgment, sentence
	ὅραμα	a sight, vision [panorama]
	πάθημα	suffering, passion [pathetic]
	πνεῦμα	wind, spirit [pneumatic]
	σῶμα	body [somatic]
	σχίσμα	dissension, division [schismatic]
	χάρισμα	free gift [charismatic]
-ος	ἔθνος	gentile, nation [ethnic]
	ἔθος	habit, custom [ethics]
	ἔτος	year
	μέρος	part, portion
	σκότος	darkness [scotoscope]
	τέλος	end, goal [telescope]

3. Nouns denoting an *agent* are formed with -της, -ευς, -γος, and -ων.

Suffix	Example	Definition
-της	δεσπότης	master, lord [despot]
	ἐργάτης	worker [energy]
	κλέπτης	thief [kleptomaniac]
	κριτής	judge [critic]
	μαθητής	learner, disciple [mathematics]

	προφήτης	prophet
	στρατιώτης	soldier [strategy]
	ψεύστης	liar [pseudonym]
-ευς	ἁλιεύς	fisherman
	ἀρχιερεύς	chief priest, high priest
	βασιλεύς	king [basilica]
	γονεύς	parent, begetter
	γραμματεύς	scribe, secretary [grammarian]
	ἱερεύς	priest
	φονεύς	murderer
-γος	ἀρχηγός	leader, ruler, founder
	ἀρχισυνάγωγος	leader of the synagogue
	γεωργός	farmer, one who works (ἐργέω) the land (γῆ)
	στρατηγός	captain, general
-ων	ἄρχων	ruler, chief [monarchy]
	ἡγεμών	leader, prince [hegemony]

4. Abstract nouns denoting *quality* or *condition* are formed with -ια, -συνη, and -ος.

Suffix	Example	Definition
-ια	ἀκαθαρσία	uncleanness, impurity
	ἁμαρτία	sin [hamartiology]
	ἐξουσία	authority, power, might
	κοινωνία	fellowship, sharing [koinonia]
	σοφία	wisdom [sophisticated]
-συνη	ἀγαθωσύνη	goodness
	δικαιοσύνη	righteousness
	ταπεινοφροσύνη	humility, modesty
-ος	βάθος	depth [bathosphere]
	ἔλεος	mercy, pity, compassion
	κράτος	strength, might [aristocracy]

5. Nouns denoting *place* are formed with -τηριον, -ων, and -ειον.

Suffix	Example	Definition
-τηριον	δεσμωτήριον	prison, jail, place of binding (δέω)
	θυσιαστήριον	altar, place of sacrifice (θυσία)
	ποτήριον	a cup, a place of drinking (ποτίζω)

	πραιτώριον	residence [Praetorium]
-ων	ἀγών	place of contest, struggle [agony]
	ἀμπελών	vineyard
	ἐλαιών	olive tree, orchard [vaseline]
	πυλών	porch, gateway
-ειον	μνημεῖον	monument, tomb [memorial]
	ταμεῖον	storeroom, secret room

6. Nouns denoting *characteristic* or *condition* are formed with -ολος.

Suffix	Example	Definition
-ολος	ἀμαρτωλός	sinner [hamartiology]
	ἀπόστολος	sent one, apostle, envoy [apostle]
	διάβολος	accuser, slanderer [diabolic]
	διδάσκαλος	teacher [didactic]
	εἴδωλον	image, idol [idol]

7. Diminutive nouns denoting *smallness* or *affection* are formed with -ιον and -ισκος (-ισκη).

Suffix	Example	Definition
-ιον	ἀρνίον	little lamb
	βιβλίον	paper, roll, book [Bible]
	θηρίον	wild beast
	κοράσιον	young girl
	νήπιον	infant, child
	παιδίον	infant, child [pediatrics]
-ισκος	νεανίσκος	young man
	παιδίσκη	maid-servant, girl slave

The following list enumerates some of the *adjective suffixes*:

1. Adjectives meaning *full of* are formed with -ρος, -ρα, and -ρον.

Suffix	Example	Definition
-ρος	πονηρός	evil, wicked
	φανερός	visible, manifest [phantasm]

2. Adjectives meaning *belonging to* or *possessing* are formed with -ιος, -ια, and -ιον.

Suffix	Example	Definition
-ιος	δεξιός	right, right side [dexterous]
	μακάριος	blessed, happy
	νήπιος	childish
	πλούσιος	wealthy, rich [plutocrat]

3. Adjectives with *perfect passive participle* meaning or expressing *possibility* are formed with -τος, -τη, and -τον.

Suffix	Example	Definition
-τος	ἀγαπητός	beloved, dear
	ἀδυνατός	powerless, weak
	δυνατός	possible, able, strong [dynamic]
	ἐκλεκτός	chosen, elect
	κλητός	called, invited
	κρυπτός	hidden, concealed [cryptic]
	πιστός	trusted, faithful

4. Adjectives used as *nouns* are formed with -λος, -λη, and -λον.

Suffix	Example	Definition
-λος	ἁμαρτωλός	sinner [hamartiology]
	τυφλός	blind, a blind man [typhlosis]
	φιλός	friendly, a friend [philanthropic]
	χωλός	lame, halt

5. Adjectives expressing a *quality* are formed with -ης and -ες.

Suffix	Example	Definition
-ης	ἀσθενής	weak, sick [neurasthenia]
	πλήρης	filled, full
	ὑγιής	healthy [hygiene]

6. Adjectives expressing *characteristic* or *tendency* are formed with -ικος, -ικη, and -ικον.

Suffix	Example	Definition
-ικος	πνευματικός	spiritual [pneumatic]

νομικός   pertaining to the law, a lawyer
σαρκικός   carnal, fleshly [sarcasm]

7. Adjectives denoting *material* are formed with -ινος, -ινη, and -ινον.

Suffix	Example	Definition
-ινος	ἀληθινός	real, true
	σάρκινος	fleshly, carnal

The following list enumerates some of the *verb suffixes*.

1. Verbs denoting an *action* or *state* are formed with -άω, -έω, and -εύω.

Suffix	Example	Definition
-άω	γεννάω	I beget [genetic]
	ζάω	I live, exist [zoo]
	κοπιάω	I toil, work
	νικάω	I conquer [Nicholas]
-έω	λαλέω	I speak [glossolalia]
	ποιέω	I do, act [poem]
-εύω	θεραπεύω	I treat, heal [therapeutic]
	προφητεύω	I prophesy [prophecy]
	φονεύω	I kill

2. Verbs expressing *causation* are formed with -όω, -αίνω, -ύνω, and -ίζω.

Suffix	Example	Definition
-όω	φανερόω	I cause to be seen, make manifest
	σταυρόω	I crucify
-αίνω	ποιμαίνω	I shepherd, feed a flock
-ύνω	αἰσχύνω	I make ashamed, disappoint
-ίζω	κτίζω	I create, bring into being
	ποτίζω	I give a drink to, water
	φωτίζω	I illumine, enlighten [photograph]

3. Verbs denoting *forcible* or *repeated* action are formed with -άζω.

Suffix	Example	Definition
-άζω	ἐργάζομαι	I work
	κράζω	I cry out, scream
	σπουδάζω	I hasten
	χορτάζω	I feed, eat

4. Verbs denoting the *beginning* of an action are formed with -σκω.

Suffix	Example	Definition
-σκω	ἀρέσκω	I come to please, satisfy
	ἐπιγινώσκω	I come to know, recognize
	εὑρίσκω	I find, discover

The following list enumerates some of the *adverb suffixes*.

1. Adverbs denoting *place where* are formed with -ι, -σι, and -ου.

Suffix	Example	Definition
-ι	ἐκεῖ	there
-σι	πέρυσι	last year
-ου	ὅπου	where
	πανταχοῦ	everywhere

2. Adverbs denoting *place whence* (from where) are formed with -θεν.

Suffix	Example	Definition
-θεν	ἄνωθεν	from above
	ἐντεῦθεν	from this place
	πόθεν	from where

3. Adverbs denoting *direction whither* (to where) are formed with -δε and -σε.

Suffix	Example	Definition
-δε	ἐνθάδε	hither (from here)
-σε	ἐκεῖσε	thither (from here)

4. Adverbs denoting *time* are formed with -τε.

Suffix	Example	Definition
-τε	ὅτε	when
	πότε	at some time
	τότε	then

5. Adverbs denoting *manner* are formed with -ως.

Suffix	Example	Definition
-ως	δικαίως	righteously
	ταχέως	quickly

6. Adverbs denoting *number* are formed with -ις and -κις.

Suffix	Example	Definition
-ις	δίς	twice
	τρίς	thrice
-κις	πολλάκις	many times

Root morphemes

Root morphemes are also derivational elements of language. In Greek they frequently function as word nuclei to which affixes are added. The meaning of a root is not always clear-cut. In the word διαλέγομαι ("I dispute"), for example, the root λεγ could mean "gather, pick," as in ἐκλέγομαι ("I pick out"), or it could mean "say, speak," as in λέγω ("I speak"). A discussion concerning how to analyze such problems seems less fruitful than learning how root morphemes function in Greek as well as the lexical meaning of as many primitive roots as possible. It is this combination of knowledge of root morphemes, plus an understanding of how morphemes fit together with derivational and inflectional affixes, that builds language fluency.

A. T. Robertson has estimated that the number of roots in Koine Greek is not more than 400, probably less. The number of different roots in New Testament Greek would, of course, be only a fraction of this figure because its total vocabulary (about 5,400 words) is much smaller than that found in the entire Greek language (about 90,000 words). When you consider that a ten-year-old child knows about 5,000 different English words, acquiring a working vocabulary of New Testament words should not be an insurmountable task.

A few common Greek root morphemes are listed below. A more complete collection can be found in part 2 of Bruce Metzger's *Lexical Aids for Students of New Testament Greek*, to which this section is indebted.

Root	Meaning	Example	Definition
ἀγ	lead, drive, weight	ἄγω	I lead
		ἐξάγω	I lead out
		ἐπισυνάγω	I gather together at one place
		ἀγρός	field (where the cattle are *led*)
		ἡγέομαι	I think, regard (*lead* through the mind)
		ἄξιος	worthy (of equal *weight*)
		ἀξίως	worthily
ἀγ	reverence	ἅγιος	holy
		ἁγιάζω	I make holy, sanctify
		ἁγιασμός	sanctification
		ἁγνίζω	I make pure
βα	go	ἀναβαίνω	I go up
		καταβαίνω	I go down
		προβαίνω	I go forward
		πρόβατον	a sheep (that which *goes forward*)
		βῆμα	judgment seat (that which a judge *gets on*)
βαλ	throw	βάλλω	I throw
		ἐκβάλλω	I cast out
		λιθοβολέω	I kill by casting stones
		διάβολος	the accuser, the devil (one who *throws* words at)
		καταβολή	foundation (that which is *thrown* down)
γεν	beget, become	γίνομαι	I become, happen, am
		γονεύς	parent
		γένος	race

		μονογενής	only, unique
		γενεά	generation
		γένεσις	birth, origin
		γένημα	fruit, produce
		γεννάω	I beget
δο	give	δίδωμι	I give
		ἐπιδίδωμι	I give to
		παραδίδωμι	I hand over, betray
		παράδοσις	tradition (that which is handed down)
		δωρεά	gift
		δωρεάν	freely
		δῶρον	gift
θαν	die	ἀποθνήσκω	I die
		θάνατος	death
		θανατόω	I put to death
		θνητός	liable to death, mortal
θε	put, place	τίθημι	I put, place
		ἐπιτίθημι	I lay upon
		περιτίθημι	I place around, clothe
		ἀθετέω	I reject
		θεμέλιος	foundation (that which is put down)
		θεμελιόω	I lay a foundation
		ἀποτίθημι	I lay aside
		ἀποθήκη	storehouse, barn
		ἀνάθεμα	a curse (that which is put aside for destruction)
καλ	call	καλέω	I call
		κλητός	called
		κλῆσις	an invitation, a call
		ἐκκλησία	church, the Church
		παρακαλέω	I beseech, exhort (I call beside myself)
		παράκλησις	exhortation, consolation
		συνκαλέω	I call together, assemble
λυ	loose	λύω	I loose
		ἀπολύω	I release, loose from
		ἀπολύτρωσις	redemption, releasing
		καταλύω	I lodge (after loosing my clothing)

		παραλύομαι	I am a paralytic (I am *unstrung*)
		παραλυτικός	paralytic
πετ	fly, fall	πέτομαι	I fly
		πετεινά	birds
		καταπέτασμα	veil, curtain
		πίπτω	I fall
		ἐκπίπτω	I fall away
		πτέρυξ	wing
		πτῶμα	corpse, fallen body
		παράπτωμα	sin, trespass (a *fall* beside)
στρεφ	turn	στρέφω	I turn
		ἀναστρέφω	I return, turn to
		ὑποστρέφω	I return
ταγ	arrange, order	τάσσω	I arrange, order
		ἐπιτάσσω	I command
		ἐπιταγή	command, order
		ὑποτάσσω	I subject (*arrange* under)
		τάξις	arrangement, order
φερ	bear, carry	φέρω	I bear, carry
		ἀποφέρω	I carry off
		διαφέρω	I differ (I *bear* apart)
		εἰσφέρω	I bring into
		προσφέρω	I bring to, offer
		προσφορά	offering
		φορέω	I bear, carry
		καρποφορέω	I bear fruit
		φορτίον	burden, load
χαρ	rejoice	χαίρω	I rejoice
		συγχαίρω	I rejoice with
		χαρά	joy
		χάρις	grace, favor
		χαρίζομαι	I give freely, forgive
		χάρισμα	gift
		εὐχαριστέω	I give thanks
		εὐχαριστία	thanksgiving

Compounds

In addition to the root plus affix method, Greek words can be constructed through the combination of two or more roots, each of which may be a free morpheme. Such a word is called a compound. Α προφήτης ("prophet") who is ψευδής ("false") is a ψευδοπροφήτης, just as a δεσπότης ("master") of an οἶκος ("house") is an οἰκοδεσπότης.

Many compounds are semantically as well as morphologically compounded. That is, the meanings of the two root morphemes determine the meaning of the compound. Anyone seeing the form νομοδιδάσκαλος ("teacher of the law") could make an intelligent guess as to what it meant if he knew the meaning of νόμος and διδάσκαλος. Other compounds are *idiomatic*. Their roots do not reveal their meaning. One has to know that ὑπάγω means "I depart." The meaning cannot be derived from analysis into ὑπό ("under") and ἄγω ("I lead"). Idiomatic compounds often result from language change in which one root becomes obsolete or takes on a modified meaning, as in ἀναβλέπω, "I receive sight" (lit. "I see up/again").

Compound words in Greek are formed in several ways. One of the most important is the prefixing of one or more prepositions. This method of compounding produces a large class of compound verbs, including, for example, διαπορεύομαι ("I go through"), εἰσπορεύομαι ("I go into"), ἐκπορεύομαι ("I go out"), and παραπορεύομαι ("I go by")—all compounds of πορεύομαι, "I go." Some prepositions used as prefixes bear a meaning that they may once have had when used separately as adverbs, but have since lost. For instance, διά sometimes introduces the idea of dividing, as in διαδίδωμι ("I distribute"), suggesting that it once meant "between." In addition, a number of prepositions are used to intensify the meaning of the simple verb. In the New Testament we find such forms as κατακαίομαι ("I burn up completely"), κατεσθίω ("I devour"), ἐκθαυμάζω ("I greatly wonder"), and ἀναιρέω ("I destroy utterly"). Almost every Greek preposition can be used with this intensifying effect (cf. the wide range of English prepositions that may be used with the same effect: *burn up, carry off, eat up, follow through, speak out*). At times the preposition provides the basis for puns and word plays that are often lost in translation. In 2 Thessalonians 3:11, for example, Paul exhorts those who are "busybodies" (περιεργαζομένους) to be "busy" (ἐργαζομένους) about their work.

Other Greek compounds—mostly nouns and adjectives—are formed by means of the combination of two or more noun stems or verb stems. This class of compounds may be divided into two principal groups. In *descriptive compounds*, the first part modifies or delimits the second part, as in μακροθυμία, "long-suffering," ὀλιγόπιστος, "having little faith," and πρωτότοκος, "firstborn." In these cases the first element describes the second element, standing in a *predicate* relationship to it. In *objective compounds*, the first element stands in a *case* relationship to the second. When the two elements are expressed in English as separate words, the first is put in an oblique case, either directly or by means of a preposition. Notice carefully the following examples.

οἰκοδεσπότης	master (δεσπότης) *of* a house (οἶκος).
πατροπαράδοτος	handed down (παραδίδωμι) *from* the fathers (πατήρ).
γονυπετής	falling (πίπτω) *on* the knees (γόνυ).
θεόπνευστος	inspired (πνέω) *by* God (θεός).
φωσφόρος	bringing (φέρω) *light* (φῶς).

It is interesting to note that what was presumably the limited vocabulary of a small Hellenic community was adapted to the needs of a worldwide empire less by borrowing or by the introduction of new words than by the adaptation of existing words through the addition of affixes or through compounding.

The Inflectional System

Most Greek words contain one or more morphemes that convey grammatical information about the word. These morphemes are called *inflectional morphemes*. Like inflections in English (cf. *go/goes, girl/girl's*), these are primarily markers of grammatical relations among words in a sentence. They do not alter either the syntactic category or the basic meaning of the stems to which they are attached. The main importance of inflectional morphemes lies at the level of sentence structure and sentence meaning, rather than at the level of word structure and word meaning.

Inflected words may be subdivided into those which are declined, namely nouns, adjectives, and pronouns, and those which are conjugated, namely verbs (including participles). The word *decline* comes from the Latin verb *declino*, "I bend away from," referring to the bending of inflection of the endings of the noun in its different cases. The word *conjugate* comes from *coniungo*, "I unite together," and means putting into order the related forms of the verb. Uninflected words, on the other hand, consist only in single

morphemes. These are usually simple connectives such as conjunctions (e.g., καί, γάρ), prepositions (e.g., ἐν, πρό), or adverbs
(e.g., νῦν, πάλιν).

Verb morphology

Because it is more complicated, let us first consider the subject
of verb morphology. The most thorough and valuable study of
New Testament Greek morphology to be published in recent
years is the grammar by Ward Powers, which explains basic
concepts and essential terminology. Although the morphological
system devised by Powers is by no means the only linguistically
acceptable one—and I have modified and simplified it for the
beginning student—it serves its purpose well, and more and more
language teachers are using it as a model for structural linguistics.
Instead of attempting to define each and every inflectional process,
we shall simply look at some of the major characteristics of Greek
verb morphology, beginning with the two basic types of verb
morphemes: lexical and inflectional morphemes.

Each form of the verb is constructed upon a basic stem, to
which are added other morphemes that indicate each relevant
detail of information about it in a given sentence. This stem is
called the *lexical morpheme* since it conveys the lexical meaning of
the verb. In Greek, the lexical morpheme of a verb is always a
bound form because it cannot exist without inflectional morphemes attached to it. Thus λύετε consists of the lexical morpheme
λυ plus the ending -ετε; λυ cannot exist independently as a
separate word. When the ending is dropped, we obtain the *present
stem*. If the endings of the present tense are added to this stem, we
have the paradigm of the verb in the present tense: λύω, λύεις,
λύει, λύομεν, λύετε, λύουσι. In this respect the lexical morpheme is
like a numeral. The numeral 1, for example, can have an unlimited
range of meaning beyond its basic meaning "one," depending
upon what other numerals, and how many, are used with it in the
complete number.

Verbs in both English and Greek may also be defined as
inflectional words whose inflected forms convey certain grammatical
categories. In English these categories are *person, number,* and *tense.*
For example, the English verb *talk* has the form *talks* in which the
morpheme -*s* indicates third person, singular number, and present
tense. Similarly, the verb *talk* has the form *talked,* in which the
morpheme represented by -*ed* indicates past time.

The inflectional system of Greek verbs is much more complicated, of course; inflectional morphemes serve to indicate not only
person, number, and tense, but also grammatical categories such
as *mood, voice,* and *aspect,* which are indicated in English by syntactic
devices. For example, English uses separate words to express
durative action in past time ("I was loosing"), but Greek can use a
single verb form for this aspect of action (ἔλυον). Likewise, the
single Greek word λύσομαι corresponds to "I shall loose myself"
in English.

In referring to these modifications, the beginning student is
usually content to speak of *prefixes* and *suffixes,* of *endings,* and (more
generally) of *inflections.* These somewhat vague terms suffice for
most purposes, but it is sometimes advantageous to use more
precise terminology based on linguistic principles. A detailed explanation is beyond the scope of this book. In general, however,
the inflectional morphemes of the Greek verb may be classified as
additive morphemes, process morphemes, and *zero morphemes.* These terms
identify verb forms that result basically from the addition of
morphemes to stems and also from the operation of specific
processes of change upon them.

For example, λύω is augmented by the addition of the affix ἐ in
front of the stem (as in ἔλυον), while ἀκούω is augmented by the
process of lengthening the initial vowel (as in ἤκουον). As both
changes have identical significance (indicating past time), they are
two allomorphs of the Greek "past time morpheme." But the first
augment is an affix, an additive morpheme, while the second
augment involves a process of change from an initial short vowel
in the stem to its corresponding long vowel. Thus this latter type
of morpheme is called a process morpheme.

On the other hand, a zero morpheme exists where an affix *could*
occur but where its absence is meaningful. In English, *let* is a
lexical morpheme and *-s* is an additive morpheme in "he *lets* me
drive." Now compare the sentence with "he let me drive." Here it
is the absence of an *-s* on *let* which indicates that the verb is past
tense and not present tense. The information that the verb is past
tense is said to be indicated by the zero morpheme—that is, by
the fact that there is nothing there when there could have been.
Powers illustrates this with the Greek form ἔλυσα, which is the
first person singular of the aorist tense. It is the fact that nothing
comes after ἔλυσα that indicates the person, number, and voice of

this form. Likewise there is a zero morpheme in the third person singular of second aorist active verbs such as ἔγνω, which has a person-number morpheme in every other form of the conjugation.

In his *Course in Modern Linguistics*, Charles Hockett proposes a helpful model to explain the significance of inflectional morphemes and their arrangement in a word. He compares the various parts of an inflected word in a language like Greek to a train picking up boxcars in a freightyard. The locomotive is the stem (or lexical morpheme); the boxcars are the various inflectional morphemes, each carrying a particular load of meaning. The total load (meaning) conveyed by the entire train (verb form) depends upon which individual boxcars (morphemes) are picked up. To get the total content of the trainload of goods, you have to unload all the boxcars. Likewise, to understand a Greek verb form you must be sure to "unload" the meaning of each individual morpheme, since each morpheme of the verb form carries its own piece of information. Other models could also be suggested (like the jigsaw puzzle we used in chapter 1: only when you fit all the pieces together do you get the total meaning of the picture). But the main thing to remember is that a Greek verb is made up of many morphemes, each contributing a unit of meaning, which together convey the total meaning of the verb form in any particular sentence.

Morphological analysis of verbs

The identification of the morphemes in any given form of a Greek verb is called *morphological analysis*. Such analysis enables the reader to obtain the significance of each morpheme and thus to understand the total significance of the verb form. Each verb form may be regarded as consisting of a number of constituents, one or more of which may be zero morphemes. These constituents may be classified as lexical morphemes, past time morphemes, perfective/durative morphemes, passive voice morphemes, future time morphemes, aspect morphemes, participle specifier morphemes, final morphemes, and prepositional prefix morphemes.

As we noted above, every verb form contains a *lexical morpheme* that carries the fundamental meaning of the word. The lexical morpheme may or may not be identical with the verb root—the basic nucleus upon which all the other forms of that verb are based. The form in which the root does occur in a verb (whether this form is identical with the verb root, or has been modified) is called the verb stem. To this stem are added other morphemes, each of which conveys particular information.

In the case of λύω, a so-called *regular verb*, the stem λυ remains the same throughout the entire conjugation of the verb. Other verbs, such as βάλλω ("I throw"), are irregular and can be mastered only by learning their principal parts (cf. future βαλῶ and perfect βέβληκα). However, the phonological rules discussed in chapter 2 enable multitudes of irregular verbs to be seen as completely regular in terms of their function in the Greek language. For example, the stem of a word is sometimes modified by its phonetic environment. Thus in the form θλίβω ("I press"), the lexical morpheme appears as θλιβ; but in other forms of this same word it will appear as θλιπ (τέθλιπται), θλιμ (τέθλιμμαι), and θλιφ (τέθλιφθε). Each of these forms is the stem in that particular word form, and thus all the stems of the one word are simply variant forms, or allomorphs, of the same morpheme.

It is important to note that a lexical morpheme possesses *inherent aspect*: it is, in itself, either durative or punctiliar (aoristic) in aspect. For some Greek verbs the basic stem upon which they build their inflectional systems is the *durative verb stem* (constructed on the basis of the present tense forms). For other verbs the basic stem is the *punctiliar verb stem* (constructed on the basis of the aorist tense forms). For durative stems a *punctiliar morpheme* (usually σα) is added in forming the aorist, and for punctiliar stems a *durative morpheme* is added to form the present. Some verbs add to their basic stem both a durative morpheme to form the present, and a punctiliar morpheme to form the aorist; but most verbs add only one or the other. This means that several New Testament verbs add an extra morpheme to their verb stem in forming their durative stem (for the present and imperfect tenses). In βάλλω this durative morpheme is the second λ that is added to the verb stem βαλ. A morpheme that is placed into another morpheme in this way is an infix. The durative morpheme is the only infix that occurs in Greek; all other morphemes are prefixes, suffixes, or process morphemes. The result is that for verbs with a second aorist (such as βάλλω), the only difference between their imperfect and aorist inflections is their stem or lexical morpheme (as in ἔβαλλον and ἔβαλον). Compare also the following verbs that form their durative (present) stems by means of the addition of durative morphemes:

Lexical Morpheme	Aorist Indicative	Present Indicative	Durative Morpheme(s)
εὑρ	εὑρον	εὑρίσκω	ισκ
καμ	ἔκαμον	κάμνω	ν
λαβ	ἔλαβον	λαμβάνω	μ, αν
μαθ	ἔμαθον	μανθάνω	ν, αν

Some second aorist verbs, whose stems are inherently punctiliar, are incapable of forming a durative form, and instead have to utilize the durative forms from another defective verb. Three such verbs that are common in the New Testament are:

Lexical Morpheme	Second Aorist Indicative	Present Indicative
ἐλθ	ἦλθον	ἔρχομαι
ἰδ	εἶδον	ὁράω
εἰπ	εἶπον	λέγω

Thus in λέγω the verb stem is durative or linear, and in εἶπον the verb stem is punctiliar. According to A. T. Robertson, this matter of the "kind of action" existing in the verb stem itself, called *Aktionsart* (Ger. 'kind of action'), was prevalent before there was any idea of the later temporal development.

Notice also that in μι- verbs the present stem is formed by the affixing of a durative morpheme before the stem, and to this stem the present and imperfect endings are then added (e.g., τίθημι, stem θε; δίδωμι, stem δο). In certain verbs a ι is inserted into the present and imperfect tenses, as in βαίνω (stem βαν), and σημαίνω (stem σημαν). Some verbs even have individual lexical allomorphs in particular inflections. An example is βαλ (the stem of βάλλω), which has, by metathesis, βλα in the perfect inflection, which then is lengthened to βλη (e.g., βέβληκα, "I have thrown").

A special morpheme indicates that the action of a verb refers to past time. This is the *past time morpheme* or *augment*, which is found in Sanskrit, Iranian, Armenian, and Greek, and only in the past tenses of the indicative mood. The tenses thus affected are the aorist, the imperfect, and the pluperfect. The origin of the augment has never been explained, although it is generally thought to have been an independent adverb, later added to the verb stem itself.

The augment has several allomorphs. If the verb stem begins with a consonant, it has in the past tenses an additive morpheme in the form of a prefixed ἐ-, called the *syllabic augment*, as in λύω, imperfect ἔλυον. If the verb stem begins with a short vowel (including a short vowel in a short diphthong), the augment consists of a process morpheme called the *temporal augment*, which lengthens the short vowel to the corresponding long vowel, as in ἐλπίζω, imperfect ἤλπιζον. A verb commencing with a long vowel or long diphthong has a *zero morpheme augment*, as in εἰρηνεύω, imperfect εἰρήνευον.

Some verbs take a *double augment*—both an additive and a process morpheme. Thus ἄγω reduplicates its first syllable and then takes the temporal augment, producing the form ἤγαγον in the aorist indicative. Similarly ἀνοίγω has the form ἀνέῳξα in the aorist active indicative (as well as in some other forms). Compound verbs that have two prefixed prepositions sometimes take an augment after each, as in ἀπεκατέστη, aorist active indicative of ἀποκαθίστημι (see Mark 8:25).

A special type of inflectional process, commonly known as *reduplication*, involves the repetition of a part or the whole of the stem within the same word. *Complete reduplication* involves the entire underlying form (e.g., Eng. *tom-tom* and *choo-choo*). When only a part of the underlying form is repeated *partial reduplication* occurs. Ancient Greek offers the best illustration of this latter process, although partial reduplication also occurs sporadically in Latin (e.g., *cano*, "I sing," but *cecini*, "I sang"; *fallo*, "I deceive," but *fefelli*, "I deceived").

Greek has two basic types of reduplication. In *perfective reduplication*, the reduplicating syllable consists of the initial consonant of the verb stem plus the vowel ε, as in λύω, λέλυκα; here the λε is an additive morpheme. Sometimes the reduplication takes the form of the syllabic augment ε-, as in ζητέω, ἐζήτηκα. If a verb begins with a short vowel or short diphthong, the reduplication appears as the temporal augment (a process morpheme), as in ἐλπίζω, ἤλπικα. When a verb commences with a long vowel or long diphthong, the verb has the zero morpheme for perfect reduplication, as in ὑστερέω, ὑστέρηκα.

Perfective reduplication in Greek is found in the perfect and pluperfect tenses, where it is an integral part of the tense stem in all moods (unlike the augment, which can appear only in the indicative). Reduplication in the perfect/pluperfect system reflects an effort to express the idea of completion or *perfective aspect* in the verb form. According to historical linguists, this effort to denote perfective aspect through the reduplication of the initial consonant goes back to Indo-European, the early ancestor of Greek (see chapter 6).

Several New Testament verbs form their present and imperfect tenses in the same manner as perfective reduplication, but using ι rather than ε as the reduplicating vowel. This is seen most clearly in μι-verbs such as δίδωμι and τίθημι. These verbs are said to contain *durative reduplication*. Historically, it appears that reduplication began with certain aorists (such as ἤγαγον), continued with some presents (such as δίδωμι), and then was taken over by the perfect tense. It is absent in the modern Greek vernacular, which (like English) forms the perfect tense by the auxiliary verb ἔχω, as in ἔχω ἀκούσει, "I have heard."

A morpheme can be affixed to the verb stem to indicate that the verb is in the passive voice. By itself, this *passive voice morpheme* is inherently aorist but can be switched to future passive if followed by the future time morpheme. The passive voice morpheme is represented by the following allomorphs:

1. In verbs with direct inflection passives, passive voice is indicated by -ε- (in the participle, subjunctive, optative) or -η- (in all other moods), as in γράφεις (aorist passive participle) and ἐγράφην (aorist passive indicative), from γράφω.

2. In all other verbs, passive voice is indicated by -θε- (in the participle, subjunctive, optative) or -θη- (in all other moods), as in λύθεις (aorist passive participle) and ἐλύθην (aorist passive indicative), from λύω.

When the *future time morpheme* is present in a verb it indicates that the action of the verb refers to future time. This morpheme is represented by several allomorphs:

1. For most Greek verbs, the future stem is formed by adding σ to the present stem (before the present tense endings). Thus the only difference between the present and future tense forms of many verbs is that the future tense forms contain the future time morpheme, as in λύω, "I loose," but λύσω, "I will loose." When the present stem ends in a consonant, amalgamation takes place, as, for example, when a stem ending in π combines with a following σ to form ψ (cf. πέμπω, future πέμψω).

2. When a stem ends in λ, μ, ν, or ρ, that verb adds ε as its

future time morpheme instead of σ. If the present stem ends in a double λ, it drops one λ, as in ἀγγέλλω, future ἀγγελέω. If the present stem contains the durative morpheme ι before λ, μ, ν, or ρ, it drops the ι, as in φαίνω, future φανέω. The future time morpheme ε then combines with the vowel of the ending into a long vowel or diphthong in accordance with the rules of contraction. Hence ἀγγελέω becomes ἀγγελῶ; φανέω becomes φανῶ.

3. Ten New Testament verbs that do not end with λ, μ, ν, or ρ are nevertheless found with ε as their future time morpheme. These verbs all end with the derivational suffix -ίζω. Thus we find ἐγγίζω, future ἐγγιέω (= ἐγγιῶ); ἐλπίζω, future ἐλπιέω (= ἐλπιῶ); μακαρίζω, future μακαριέω (= μακαριῶ).

4. Two New Testament verbs indicate future time by the zero morpheme, their inflections being added directly to the lexical morpheme: ἐσθίω (stem φαγ) becomes φάγομαι; and πίνω (stem πι) becomes πίομαι.

The most important element of tense in the Greek verb system is the kind of action being referred to. This is called *aspect* or *Aktionsart*, and it is where the major distinction between the different tenses lies. For example, there are three tenses in Greek which have the past time morpheme, that is, which indicate past time: the imperfect, the aorist, and the pluperfect. They all refer to the past; the only difference between them is the kind of action, or aspect, that they indicate. The imperfect indicates *durative* (*linear* or *progressive*) aspect (where the emphasis is upon the *duration* or *continuation* of the action). The aorist indicates *punctiliar* or *simple* aspect (where the action is viewed in its totality no matter how long it lasted). The pluperfect indicates perfective or completed aspect (where the consequences of a prior action are being stressed). Note that the aorist tense only has the past time morpheme in the indicative mood, since only in the indicative mood does the aorist refer to past time. Otherwise, in the subjunctive, imperative, infinitive, or participle the aorist refers to punctiliar aspect, in contrast with the present, which designates durative aspect.

In our discussion of the lexical morpheme, we noted that each Greek verb possesses inherent aspect, either punctiliar or durative. Yet in addition to its inherent aspect, a verb is capable of showing aspect by means of certain *aspect morphemes* that indicate kind of action. Notice the following:

1. A large number of verbs in the New Testament indicate punctiliar aspect by the addition of the *punctiliar morpheme* (σα [before consonants] or σ [before vowels]) to the ending of the word, as in λύομεν, ἐλύσαμεν. The punctiliar morpheme has two important allomorphs: α, found in verbs whose stems end in λ, μ, ν, or ρ, as in μένω, ἔμεινα; and κα, found in certain μι- verbs, such as δίδωμι, ἔδωκα.

2. Perfective aspect is indicated by the addition of the *perfective morpheme* (κ [before vowels], κε [before the infinitive morpheme ναι], κει [for the pluperfect active form], or κα [in most other forms]). Thus λύω, "I loose," but λέλυκα, "I have loosed." This perfective morpheme is found only in the *active voice*. In the middle and passive voices, perfective aspect is indicated by perfective reduplication alone.

3. There is no durative aspect morpheme. Thus in the λύω paradigm, no morpheme is added to the verb to indicate durative aspect in the present and imperfect tenses. Instead, the *neutral morpheme* is used. The neutral morpheme is always o or ε—o when the ending begins with a nasal (μ, ν) or with υ; ε in all other cases. This morpheme simply fills the aspect slot without conveying any meaning—hence the term *neutral morpheme*. If a verb is inherently punctiliar and a durative form is required, a durative morpheme will be added (as in δίδωμι, stem δο), or a durative infix will be inserted into the lexical morpheme (as in βαίνω, stem βαν). In the subjunctive mood, the neutral morpheme o/ε lengthens to ω/η; that is, the subjunctive mood is formed by a process morpheme, not an additive morpheme. In the optative mood, the morpheme ι is added to the aspect morpheme (in the passive voice, ιη is added to the passive morpheme). This always results in a diphthong: in the present this produces οι (as in λύοιμι, "I would be loosing"); in the first aorist active and middle, σαι (as in λύσαιμι, "I would loose"); and in the aorist passive, θειη (as in λυθείην, "I would be loosed").

Certain morphemes specify that forms in which they occur are participles. Examples of *participle specifier morphemes* follow:

1. The morpheme -ντ- is the formative element of all active participles (except the perfect) and of the passive participles of the first and second aorist. Thus we have λύοντες (present active participle), λύσαντες (aorist active participle), and λυθέντες (aorist passive participle).
2. The morpheme -μεν- is the formal element in all middle and passive (except aorist) participles; for example, λυόμενος (present middle/passive participle) and λυσάμενος (aorist middle participle).
3. The perfect active participle is formed in the following ways: with -υια- in the feminine gender; -ος in the nominative masculine/neuter singular; and -οτ- otherwise. Hence the forms λελυκώς (from λελυκοτς), λελυκυῖα, λελυκός.

Every verb must, of course, have an ending, or a *final morpheme*: the *person-number morpheme*, if the verb is indicative, subjunctive, optative, or imperative; the *infinitive morpheme*, if it is an infinitive; or the *case-number morpheme*, if it is a participle.

The person-number morpheme has a wide range of forms and allomorphs that can be found in any Greek grammar. Person-number morphemes normally also indicate voice: -μεν indicates first person plural active voice while -μεθα indicates first person plural middle or passive voice. Some person-number morphemes indicate past time or non-past time as well: -ντο is past time, and -νται is non-past time (present or future). Again, -κα- indicates active voice as well as perfective aspect. A morpheme that conveys multiple information is called a *multiple morpheme*.

Another final morpheme, the infinitive morpheme, has the following allomorphs: -ειν in the present and future active; -αι in the aorist active; -ναι in the aorist passive; and -σθαι elsewhere.

The Greek participle is formed from the appropriate tense stem by the addition of the appropriate participle specifier morpheme and the case-number morpheme. The case-number morpheme will be the appropriate morpheme from the participle declension paradigm.

A large number of New Testament verbs are compound verbs, words composed of a *simplex* verb and a preposition that has been added to it. The prepositional prefix interacts with the verb stem to produce the lexical meaning of the compound. As we have seen, sometimes this is a recognizable combination of meanings, and sometimes it is a new meaning quite distinct from that of its components. Occasionally a verb that begins with prepositionlike phonemes is treated as a compound verb even though its phonemes belong in fact to the verb's lexical morpheme. Thus in the New Testament διακονέω is treated as a compound of δία and κονέω (and augmented as in διηκόνει, Mark 1:31) although it is not.

A compound verb will therefore contain an extra additive morpheme—the *prepositional prefix morpheme*. The augment comes after the prefix and immediately before the stem. Thus the imperfect indicative of συνβάλλω is συνέβαλλον, not ἐσυνβαλλον. The final vowel of a preposition is elided (except in the case of περί and πρό) when the verb is augmented. A few verbs have no simplex (uncompounded form): compare the common verb ἀποκτείνω, "I kill"; κτείνω is not found in the New Testament.

To summarize, all the information about the total meaning of a particular verb form in Greek is conveyed through the morphemes of which it is composed. There are altogether nine categories or morphemes that can occur in a verb. The places where these morphemes can occur are called *morpheme slots*. It is important for you to be able to recognize each morpheme and to determine the information that it contains.

The most helpful way of understanding the process of Greek morphological analysis is by working through a number of examples. The selection of forms from λύω in figure 7 provides an opportunity for this. Examine each form, identify what it is, and then work out its meaning. Where a morpheme consists of the lengthening of a phoneme, this is indicated by a capital *L* in the column for that morpheme. A zero morpheme is indicated by the symbol # in the appropriate column (e.g., when the person-number morpheme is attached directly to the stem λυ to form the perfect middle/passive; that verb will contain no aspect morpheme, and it is this fact that will indicate that it is perfect, as in λέλυμαι).

Morphological analysis of nouns

Nouns, adjectives, pronouns, articles, and participles indicate their case and number by inflectional endings. Where the same pattern of endings is used by words, that pattern is called a paradigm (Gk. παράδειγμα, 'example'). Nouns in Greek comprise

Figure 7 Verb Forms of λύω

Verb Form	Prepositional Prefix	Past Time	Perfective/ Durative	Lexical	Passive Voice	Future Time	Aspect	Participle	
								Specifier	Final
λύω				λυ			ο		ω
λύει				λυ			ε		ι
λύομεν				λυ			ο		μεν
λύσει				λυ		σ	ε		ι
ἐλύομεν		ἐ		λυ			ο		μεν
ἔλυε(ν)		ἐ		λυ			#		ε(ν)
ἐλύσαμεν		ἐ		λυ			σα		μεν
ἔλυσα		ἐ		λυ			σα		#
λελύκαμεν			λε	λυ			κα		μεν
λέλυμαι			λε	λυ			#		μαι
λελυκέναι			λε	λυ			κε		ναι
ἐλύθησαν		ἐ		λυ	θη		σα		ν
λῦσαι				λυ			σα		αι
λύσωμεν				λυ			ω		μεν
λυθησόμεθα				λυ	θη	σ	ο		μεθα
λυθῇ				λυ	θ(ε)		η		ι
λυόμενοι				λυ			ο	μεν	οι
καταλύονται	κατα			λυ			ο		νται
κατελύομεν	κατ(α)	ἐ		λυ			ο		μεν
λυσαμένων				λυ			σα	μεν	ων
λύωσι				λυ			ω		σι

three declensions, each of which contains a number of paradigms. In declension, adjectives, pronouns, articles, and participles follow the analogy of nouns and so do not entail a separate discussion.

There are two ways in which Greek adds the case-number suffix to produce forms: (1) with a *stem formative*, or (2) directly to the root or stem. Nouns of the first and second declensions add, respectively, the stem formatives -α- and -ο- to their roots to form their stems. Thus, for example, ἡμέραν consists of the lexical morpheme ἡμερ- and the stem formative -α-. The stem formative is not a separate morpheme, as it does not independently convey a distinct meaning. The noun therefore contains only two morphemes, the lexical morpheme and the case-number morpheme. (This is in distinction to the view of Goetchius that the stem formative is in fact a morpheme.) The stem formative is usually taken in conjunction with the case-number suffix, so that the two constitute the ending of a noun: ἡμέραν is thus ἡμερ-, word root, and -αν, ending. Similarly the root of κύριος is κυρι-, and the ending -ος is added to indicate case and number.

The stem formative may undergo modification in certain phonetic environments. Some first declension nouns lengthen the stem formative -α- to -η- throughout the singular, and a few lengthen the -α- to -η- in the genitive and dative singular only (cf. ζωή, ζωῆς; δόξα, δόξης). There are also some differences between masculine and feminine forms, resulting in the five paradigms of the first declension. The case-number suffix for the nominative singular of the feminine paradigms is the zero morpheme—that is, it is the absence of any case-number suffix that serves to identify the form as nominative singular. In the second declension, the stem formative -ο- lengthens to -ω- in the dative singular and genitive plural.

Nouns that have no stem formative, but instead add the case-number suffix directly to the root, comprise the third declension. Their noun root thus also becomes their stem, which can be obtained by removing the genitive singular suffix (usually -ος, but sometimes -ως), as in σάρξ, σαρκός; root σαρκ. Nouns of the third declension fall into two categories according to whether their stem ends in a semivowel (ι̯ or υ̯) or a consonant phoneme. Consonant stems are further subdivided into paradigms by the nature of the last phoneme of the stem—that is, there are different paradigms for bilabials, alveolars, velars, and so on. Most of the paradigms of the third declension are considered regular

since their forms can be predicted on the basis of regular phonological rules; only in a small number of words are alternative
ways used for handling the conjunction of stem and suffix.

The student will find third declension nouns more difficult to
master than either the first or second declension. This is due to
the great variety of their stems. There are, however, constant
features in their endings. The genitive singular always ends in ς
(and ος most frequently); the dative singular in ι; the nominative,
vocative, and accusative plural of masculine and feminine nouns
end in ς (and in ες or ας most frequently); and the dative plural in
σι(ν). In general, the phonological rules that apply to verbs operate
for nouns also: a bilabial plus σ becomes ψ, an alveolar drops out
before ς, and so forth.

Since the aim of most students is to be able to recognize (and
not write) words of the third declension, it is not really necessary
to memorize all thirty or so third declension paradigms. Familiarity
with the overall patterns of some basic paradigms—the most
useful are βασιλεύς, σάρξ, γένος, and σῶμα—will increase the
likelihood of recognizing the case and number of most third
declension nouns as they are encountered.

Perhaps a greater difficulty for the beginner in Greek will be the
conflicting attitudes among scholars toward the number of cases
in Greek. Many teachers prefer the eight-case system, and some
of its adherents can become almost fanatical about its value. Yet in
Greek the genitive and the ablative are combined into one form,
and the dative, locative, and instrumental into another. Why,
then, should the same "case" be described as the "genitive of
separation" by Eric Jay and the "ablative of separation" by Dana
and Mantey?

One major reason for these inconsistencies is the distinction
some grammarians make between form and function. To Dana
and Mantey, case is a matter of function rather than of form.
However, the problem with such a system of introducing an
"ablative," a "locative," and an "instrumental," when there is
actually no distinction, is that confusion is added to something
already difficult enough. And if it is a matter of functional distinctions, why stop with eight cases? As Eugene Nida points out in
his *Linguistic Interludes*, there is a sufficient number of functional
differences for some twenty-five divisions! This means that the
eight-case system fits neither the formal nor the functional pattern

of Greek. If we decide to follow the formal pattern at least we will be right on one score.

The linguistics student should not consider these apparent inconsistencies as difficulties so much as sources for understanding the many ways in which the complex phenomena of language can be examined, conceptualized, and discussed. Linguists should no more be expected to agree on every point than should political historians be expected to agree concerning the causes of the Civil War. Actually, this ambiguity about language is also its strength, for we can use it to help us realize that there is no one, final system of Greek grammar, just as there are no simple, ultimate answers to most complex questions concerning human activity. Despite differences among grammarians there are many points of agreement, and each can learn something from the other.

Why Study Morphology?

Students who have wrestled with the problem of maintaining an adequate vocabulary for translating the New Testament are familiar with the difficulty and frustration generally encountered in "vocabulary drill." Teachers often display a high degree of skill and enthusiasm for developing unpleasant assignments designed to expand the lexicon of their students. In my career as a college and seminary Greek teacher I can remember trying every method I could find to increase my students' meager vocabulary, from Greek-English memory cards to word lists based on frequency of occurrence. In time, however, I found certain methods of word attack that could be used effectively in the classroom, and some of the techniques could be explained on the basis of linguistic principles.

Like many other teachers before me, I quickly concluded that rote memorization is not an adequate method alone, since words that are crammed for an exam are soon forgotten unless reviewed often. This is not to imply that a word list is not a useful tool for vocabulary building. As a supplement to the study of words in context it is the student's best friend. But it is only by seeing the same word over and over in many contexts that any real depth of understanding can be achieved. This, however, is more a matter of semantics than of morphology and is discussed in greater detail in chapter 5.

In morphology, I found a more useful tool for vocabulary building. After my students had studied the structure of words, including the different types of morphemes and their various functions, they found some interesting clues to meaning in the words themselves. As their knowledge of the basic meanings of the morphemes increased, their ability to memorize and retain vocabulary increased as well.

It should become immediately apparent, for example, that πνεῦμα is a noun denoting result ("that which has been breathed or blown, spirit") because it ends with the nominalizing derivational suffix -μα. The student who has built up a vocabulary of -μα words—βάπτισμα, γράμμα, κήρυγμα, δικαίωμα—should automatically place πνεῦμα in this category. Further investigation of πνεῦμα can lead to the discovery that πνευματικός is an adjective denoting characteristic ("that which is breath-like, spiritual") because of its -ικος suffix. At the same time the student is grasping the structure of Greek words, he is building his lexicon of derivational morphemes. Each new word encountered in reading is an opportunity to add something to the list. Vocabulary might develop from πνεῦμα to πνευματικός to λογικός to λόγος to λογίζω. But at each step along the way the new morphemes—πνευ-, -μα, λογ-, -ικος, -ος, -ιζω—are classified and learned so that when encountered again they can, in combination with the context, make the learning of new words both interesting and no more complicated than necessary.

The study of English cognates and derivatives based on Indo-European roots is yet another effective method of learning vocabulary. English is a sort of reservoir of the classical languages; according to one estimate it has absorbed for its own use more than one-quarter of the entire Greek lexical stock. Take, for example, the word ἔργον. If you will look up the etymology you will find that the root is ϝεργ, meaning "to do something," seen in the word *work*. Thus ἐργάζω means "I work," and ἐργάτης is a "workman." The phonological shapes of ϝεργ and *work* are only superficially different, and by using what we know about the ways sound descended into various Indo-European languages we can explain all this. As we saw in chapter 2, the ϝ in ϝεργ represents a rounding of simple breath—the Greek digamma—and can readily disappear before a vowel. Moreover, γ is only the voiced form of *k*, so that ϝεργ and *work* are largely the same word. Even the difference in vowels can be explained: ϝεργ came through Latin with vowel gradation, so that an *organization* is something that *works*, and that when somebody *organizes* the *workers* into an *organization* he is only working the workers into something that works. Thus, knowing that ϝεργ is the word *work* in a different form will permit you to learn several words easily and remember them longer.

To summarize, rather than memorizing long lists of roots and affixes, students should come out of their study of morphology with the following summary of the structure of the Greek morphological system:

1. A lexicon of roots derived from Indo-European:

γεν	beget, become
θαν	die
καλ	call

2. Combinations of roots (compounds) that form stems:

ψευδοπροφήτης	false prophet
οἰκοδεσπότης	master of a house
ἐκπορεύομαι	I go out

3. Derivational prefixes added to these stems to give additional meaning:

ἀτιμία	dishonor (not-honoring)
εὐλογία	blessing (well-spoken of)
ἡμιθανής	half-dead

4. Derivational suffixes added to indicate part of speech and to modify meaning:

φονεύς	murderer (one who murders)
σαρκικός	carnal (pertaining to the flesh)
φανερόω	I manifest (I cause to be seen)

5. Inflectional affixes added to account for such factors as person, number, case, aspect, and voice:

ἀνθρώπῳ	for a man

λυσόμεθα   we will loose ourselves
λύσατε   loose!

Of course many fascinating exceptions and modifications will present themselves. For example, recent studies of κρίσις and κρίμα raise the question as to whether -σις sometimes extends its meaning to overlap with that of -μα, especially in the Gospel of John. This merely shows that not every morpheme has a distinct and absolute significance. Indeed, we will see in chapter 4 that word formation does not necessarily give the full meaning or even the correct meaning of a word as it is actually used. But meanwhile we may be confident that morphemes are the minimal units of meaning out of which meaningful utterances are built in ways still to be determined.

The examples of Greek morphemes given in this chapter, few and scattered as they are, should at least indicate something of the range and diversity of the morphological devices that have been used by Greek speakers in the course of the language's history. The possibilities of morphological arrangement are as endless as those of sound combinations.

At the same time, however, language, even in its most elementary reaches, cannot exist without syntax. Syntax, more than any aspect of language, lends itself to the purposes of connected thought and its communication. It is the essential ingredient of that elusive element called meaning. Morphology, therefore, is but a necessary prelude to the study of the ways in which speakers of a language pattern words and morphemes to serve the one essential aim of conveying meaning.

Suggestions for Further Reading

Some widely known treatments of Greek morphology are the following:

Greenlee, J. Harold. *A New Testament Greek Morpheme Lexicon*. Grand Rapids: Zondervan, 1983.

Jacques, Xavier. *List of New Testament Words Sharing Common Elements*. Rome: Biblical Institute, 1969.

Metzger, Bruce M. *Lexical Aids for Students of New Testament Greek*. Princeton, N.J.: Theological Book Agency, 1974.

Mussies, G. *The Morphology of Koine Greek as Used in the Apocalypse of St. John*. Leiden: Brill, 1971.

Nida, Eugene. *Linguistic Interludes*. Santa Ana, Calif.: Summer Institute of
    Linguistics, 1947.
Rogers, Thomas. *Greek Word Roots: A Practical List with Greek and English
    Derivatives*. Grand Rapids: Baker, 1981 [1968].

The books by Greenlee, Jacques, and Metzger are all intended
for the beginning student. The volume by Mussies is harder
reading; but it illustrates the close relationship between morphology and exegesis. Nida's *Linguistic Interludes* deals in a popular
and amusing manner with the supposed superiority of the Greek
morphological system.

For a fuller survey of the development of morphological theory,
the reader should consult Eugene A. Nida, *Morphology: The Descriptive Analysis of Words* (Ann Arbor: University of Michigan Press,
1946) and Benjamin Elson and Velma Pickett, *An Introduction to
Morphology and Syntax* (Santa Ana, Calif.: Summer Institute of Linguistics, 1965). Ward Powers's *Learn to Read the Greek New Testament*
(Grand Rapids: Eerdmans, 1979), despite its unassuming title, is a
reasonably thorough application of morphological principles to
New Testament Greek, as is Eugene Van Ness Goetchius's *The
Language of the New Testament* (New York: Charles Scribner's Sons,
1965).

4

Syntax: The Architecture of the Greek Sentence

So long ago that you have probably forgotten where it happened, you discovered that you could talk. This miraculous discovery may have taken place very early indeed, perhaps while you were still eating your meals in a high chair and getting things like chopped carrots for lunch—whereupon you probably said, as would any sensible child, "I don't want carrots. I want a cookie." If this announcement had no immediate effect on your menu, it at least had stupendous implications for your future. For you were suddenly talking in sentences—not just pronouncing a few words, but stringing them together and expressing whole thoughts. You did not know it at the time, but you had just entered the world of *syntax*.

Up to this point we have examined systematically the phonological and morphological structure of New Testament Greek. Now we shall see how words may be combined into larger syntactic units—phrases, clauses, and sentences. So far, there would be little disagreement among linguists about the basic structure of Greek. Differences of opinion might center on matters of detail: the precise number of items in the phonemic inventory of the language as described in chapter 2, for example, or the manner of dividing certain combinations into morphemes, as outlined in the last chapter. But in general, all linguists basically agree about the methodology of phonological and morphological analysis.

Disagreement becomes more obvious in the realm of syntactical analysis. Greek syntax is extraordinarily complex and can be blueprinted by various methods, none of them perfect. It would not be practical to deal here with the more traditional aspects of syntax that should be standard items in a class dealing with Greek grammar. Instead, we will give attention to general principles and, especially, to those principles that will be of use in exegesis. Some basic information is also provided on how syntactic rules can be formalized, both to suggest the kinds of problems linguists face in their thinking about sentence structure, and also to make other materials on syntax more accessible to beginning students.

Structure and Content Words

Let us begin by observing once again a fact emphasized earlier in this book: that an organized whole is greater than the sum of its parts. What this means in linguistics is that at each major step up the ladder of the linguistic hierarchy, something new emerges that was neither present nor predictable at the preceding level. Thus we have seen that when phonemes are organized into morphemes, they take on meaning, which is not a quality associated with the individual phonemes themselves, but is solely the result of the way they are combined. In the same way, when morphemes (or the groups of morphemes we call words) are combined to form utterances, a new kind of meaning emerges that is not due to the individual morphemes, but is strictly a function of the way they are combined. Linguists refer to this meaning as *structural meaning*. Structural meaning is the kind of meaning associated with the combination of morphemes or words, as opposed to *lexical meaning*, the kind of meaning associated with the separate morphemes or words. The *total linguistic meaning* of an utterance consists of the lexical meanings of the separate words it contains plus the structural meanings of the grammatical devices connecting them. Lexical meanings are to be found in dictionaries; structural meanings, however, are indicated by formal grammatical devices that are present in utterances themselves. No utterance is fully intelligible without both kinds of meaning. For example, in chapter 1 we saw that the words strung together in the phrase *language men the foreign a learned* have lexical meanings, but the utterance as a whole has no structural meaning. On the other hand, the structural meanings of the following nonsense words are clear, though the lexical meanings are obscure: "The bingest sturks were stingled by a klunny bung retingly." We can easily see that *sturks* and *bung* are nouns, for instance, or that *stingled* is a verb. The point is that separate words may be organized into a larger structure—a structure to which each word contributes without losing its own identity, and that has a structural meaning beyond the sum of the lexical meanings of the words that make it up.

This concept of lexical and structural meaning is linked to the distinction linguists make between *structure words* (also called *function words*) and *content words* (also called *form words*). We call the first group *structure words* because they are the material from which we build sentences. These are words such as articles, prepositions, and conjunctions, which have little precise lexical meaning, but which have great importance in signaling relationships among the meaningful words with which they appear. For example, the statement *Ship sails today* is confusing; we cannot interpret it because structure words are absent. But when it reads, "The ship sails today," or conversely, "Ship the sails today," we know exactly what is meant. Although the words *Ship sails today* are content words, they do not have much content until we add the mortar provided by structure words.

If structure words are the mortar of language, content words are the bricks that provide the substance of a sentence. Content class words usually have more lexical meaning. They include words such as nouns, verbs, adjectives, and adverbs. They can be interchanged with words of the same class without losing structural significance, although the meaning of the sentence changes. Every content class contains thousands of words, which can be substituted for each other in countless ways. Structure words, in contrast, have a fixed roster; new structure words are added to a language only rarely. The author of the Book of Ephesians, for example, uses content words that have not yet been traced in any Greek document of the pre-Christian period. As new things and new concepts are assimilated into a culture, new words are sometimes needed to describe them. On the other hand, you will look in vain for new conjunctions in the transition from Classical to Koine Greek.

Because they acquire meaning in a larger context, content words are structured with roots and affixes. The preceding discussion of morphology was concerned mainly with content class words, those that may contain more than one inflectional or derivational morpheme: λύω can become ἔλυσα; from καλός we can derive καλῶς;

and the intensive form of ἐσθίω is κατεσθίω. But what can you do with πῶς, πρός, or δέ?

In the linguistic approach to syntactical analysis we begin, therefore, by examining the various devices the Greek language employs to indicate structural meanings. For example, if we looked up the words ἀγαθὸν μαθητὴν ἀγαπᾷ ὁ θεός in a lexicon, we would find that ἀγαθόν corresponds to *good*, μαθητήν to *disciple*, ἀγαπᾷ to *loves*, ὁ to *the*, and θεός to *God*. Taking the Greek words as they appear, we might expect them to mean "Good disciple loves the God." Why, then, do we translate them as "God loves a good disciple"? The answer is that Greek and English, being different languages, have different structures. The lexical meanings of the Greek words are much the same as the lexical meanings of the English words; however, the structural devices which relate the Greek words to each other are entirely different from those which relate the English words to each other. Starting at the beginning (as the Greeks did, without hunting around for the subject), we learn from the morpheme -ν attached to ἀγαθόν and μαθητήν that both of these words are direct objects and also that they belong together. Similarly, the ending of ἀγαπᾷ marks it as a present tense, third person singular verb, and the -ς of θεός labels it as the subject in spite of its final position in the sentence. Thus the lexical meanings are the same in the Greek and English sentences, but the formal devices that express these meanings are not the same.

When we examine the structure of the English sentence, we find that word order plays a very important role. If the order is changed, we get either a different meaning (as in "A good disciple loves God") or else we get no structural meaning at all (as in "Loves God disciple good a"). Word order is so important in English that morphology and syntax may be said to play complementary roles in bearing the burden of meaningfulness. In highly inflected languages like Greek and Latin, however, word order plays a somewhat secondary role, though it is frequently used to indicate relative emphasis on words. Inflected languages are more rigidly bound by their morphological structures, and so preserve a modicum of syntactical freedom that may be used at will for purposes of stress, rhetorical effect, or poetic license. Notice, however, that the order of words in Greek is not completely free. In the sample sentence, the two words ὁ θεός must be kept together and in the same order; if they were to be separated, or if their order were to be changed, the resulting structure would be ungrammatical (though the meaning might still be intelligible to a native speaker).

In summary, then, structural meanings are fundamental and necessary meanings. In order to understand a sentence we must know not only what individual words mean but also what their grammatical functions are. The common notion that the study of language is merely the study of words involves a serious error. This is the misconception that words are isolated units, while longer utterances are simply mechanical combinations of the smaller units. If this were the case, then all we would have to do in studying a foreign language would be to learn the individual words and their meanings. But anyone who has actually studied a foreign language knows that this is not true. Accordingly, it is necessary to regard the morphological system, or the ways in which words are built out of morphemes, as a subsystem of syntax, which includes the ways in which words are arranged relative to each other in utterances.

Immediate Constituent Analysis

The recognition of structure and content class words is only the first step in recognizing larger structures. Because of the great variety and complexity of Greek sentences, analysis of these constructions could become bogged down in details unless some simplified method of expressing the framework of the sentence is found. Therefore, linguists apply the principle of *immediate constituent analysis* (usually abbreviated IC) in determining the interrelationships of the components (or constituents) of a sentence. This approach assumes that in any given sentence some words are more closely related than others, and that a sentence is made up of two-part constructions on a series of levels.

For example, the sentence *The good teacher walked to the classroom* consists of two main parts (ICs), namely, *the good teacher* and *walked to the classroom*. Each part, in turn, consists of two parts, and these also consist of two parts, until by cutting the sentence into smaller and smaller groups we reach the level of single words or morphemes. A complete IC analysis of the sample sentence would look something like figure 8. (Further analysis, such as *teacher* into *teach* and *-er* or *walked* into *walk* and *-ed*, is of course perfectly possible, but this would be a matter of morphology.)

Figure 8 Immediate Constituent Analysis—Phase 1

Step 1: The teacher | walked to the classroom

Step 2: The teacher | walked | to the classroom

Step 3: The | teacher | walked | to | the | classroom

Figure 9 Immediate Constituent Analysis—Phase 2

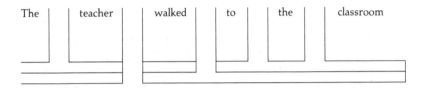

| The | teacher | walked | to | the | classroom |

This procedure gives us a rather clear picture of how a basic sentence pattern can be subdivided into its component parts until the smallest units are derived. Retrace the order of cuts in figure 8. First, separate the subject from its predicate. Then cut the sentence into constructions that have some degree of internal unity. Finally, separate the parts of the remaining unified constituents. These steps could also be represented diagrammatically, as in figure 9.

The IC analysis approach illustrates an important principle of language study and one that is particularly significant for Greek. The various parts of speech have certain "slots" into which they can be fitted. These slots, plus the classes of words that fill them, are sometimes called *tagmemes* (Gk. τάγμα, 'order, arrangement'). The tagmemic principle of grammar works on several levels. At the lowest level, that of the word, it is used to describe the morphemes making up what have been traditionally called simple and compound words. The other levels might be called the phrase level, the clause level, and the sentence level.

An example of a sentence level tagmeme is the Greek utterance ἀδελφὸς βλέπει ἄνθρωπον ("A brother sees a man"). In this sentence, three slots are immediately obvious: a subject slot, a predicate slot, and an object slot. In each of these slots many substitutions are possible. For example, not only such nouns as δοῦλος and γυνή but many other morphemes and morpheme sequences may be substituted for ἀδελφός. Thus by making certain changes in a basic sentence, it is possible to generate an infinite variety of new sentences. As the content words are replaced the meaning changes, but the structure of the sentence remains the same. A "slot-and-filler" grammar is nothing other than a means of describing ways in which these various classes of words can be used in sentences.

Greek Sentence Patterns

Turning to the Greek sentence itself, it is necessary to begin with an understanding of what a *sentence* is. The problem of defining the sentence is not a simple one (How are sentences like "Good morning!" or "Heavens!" to be accounted for?). Typical definitions of sentences may concentrate on meaning (" a group of words expressing a complete thought"), function ("a structure in a language that is not shown by some grammatical feature to be part of a larger structure"), or orthography ("a group of words beginning with a capital letter and ending with a period"). One is led to conclude that a *sentence* can only be superficially defined without a detailed analysis of its components. However, the following definition (used by many structural linguists) may be helpful: "The basic sentence is the simple declaration, having as its immediate constituents a subject and a predicate." (The structure *subject-predicate* [with fixed word order in English and variable word order in Greek] is characteristic of many sentences in both English and Greek, though there are many other sentences that have different structures.)

If all the sentences of the Greek language were reduced to their basic patterns or kernels, most Greek sentences could be represented by a comparatively small number of patterns. Not all linguists would group sentences as the following patterns suggest, but this is a common and widely used division. *Kernel sentences*, described here using traditional terminology, are limited to simple declarative forms. We will deal only with what are usually considered *complete sentences* and view the above mentioned phrases as abbreviated expressions where information is implied or supplied by the participants.

With Intransitive Verbs

Pattern 1:   (D) Noun$_{nom}$ Verb

As we have indicated, the noun-verb (subject-predicate) relationship is the basis for most Greek sentences. Pattern 1 consists

of this noun-verb combination with no other immediate constituents. The *D* in parentheses means that a *determiner* may be
present. This class includes such words as articles, possessives,
and demonstratives.

While in English the subject must be expressed, it may be
deleted in Greek since the Greek verb ending always indicates the
subject. When the subject is expressed, it is in the nominative
case, the form in which it appears in a lexicon. The subject may
occur before or after the verb; there is no need for a fixed word
order as in English since the nominative case form in which the
Greek subject appears identifies it clearly.

(*Note*: In the Greek examples used in this section of the text, the
New Testament sentences have been altered slightly for simplification; in no case, however, has the word order been changed.)

John 19:28	διψῶ	"I thirst."
John 1:50	πιστεύεις	"You believe."
John 3:8	τὸ πνεῦμα πνεῖ	"The wind blows."
John 6:61	γογγύζουσιν οἱ μαθηταί	"The disciples are complaining."
John 9:9	ἐγώ εἰμι	"I am."
John 4:53	ἐπίστευσεν	"He believed."

Pattern 2:   (D) Noun_{nom}   Verb   Adverb

Pattern 2 represents the other major pattern that can be
produced with an intransitive verb. The word class *adverb* includes
the accusative of nouns or the neuter accusative of adjectives as
well as adverbs proper.

John 4:17	καλῶς εἶπας	"You spoke well."
Luke 22:62	ἔκλαυσεν πικρῶς	"He wept bitterly."
James 4:3	κακῶς αἰτεῖσθε	"You ask amiss."

With Transitive Verbs

Pattern 3:   (D) Noun_{nom}   Verb   (D) Noun_{acc}

The second noun in this pattern is also known as the *direct object*
or the *verb completer*. The direct object answers the question,
"Whom or what does the verb affect or refer to?" A set of suffixes
in the accusative case normally signals the direct object (some
Greek verbs take their object in the dative or even the genitive

case). Nouns or pronouns may fill this slot. Again, word order in this pattern relative to the verb is free; that is, there is no fixed sequence as is the case in English.

John 19:16	παρέλαβον τὸν Ἰησοῦν	"They took Jesus."
John 19:18	αὐτὸν ἐσταύρωσαν	"They crucified him."
John 21:17	φιλῶ σε	"I love you."
John 15:9	ἠγάπησέν με ὁ πατήρ	"The Father loved me."

Pattern 4:   (D) Noun$_{nom}$ Verb   (D) Noun$_{dat}$ (D) Noun$_{acc}$

This is the indirect object-direct object pattern. The second noun answers the question, "To whom does the action occur?" or "To whom is the action directed?" The dative case signals the indirect object. Again, both nouns and pronouns may be used, and again, there is no fixed word order.

John 5:22	τὴν κρίσιν δέδωκεν τῷ υἱῷ	"He has given the Son judgment."
John 4:25	ἀναγγελεῖ ἡμῖν ἄπαντα	"He will tell us everything."
John 10:28	δίδωμι αὐτοῖς ζωὴν αἰώνιον	"I give them eternal life."

With Linking Verbs

Pattern 5:   (D) Noun$_{nom}$ L-Verb   Adjective$_{nom}$

This pattern is traditionally known as the *predicate adjective* pattern. Notice that adjectives appearing in other parts of the sentence preposed with nouns do not produce new kernel sentences but simply expand existing ones:

The child is *happy*.   (kernel sentence)
The *small* child is *happy*.   (expansion)

The most common linking verbs are εἰμί and γίνομαι, though the verb εἰμί is frequently deleted from the pattern and must be supplied in translation. The nominative case identifies the predicate relationship, and the adjective agrees with the subject.

John 17:10   τὰ ἐμὰ σά ἐστιν   "My things are yours."
Luke 2:25   ὁ ἄνθρωπος   "The man is just."
             δίκαιος

Pattern 6:   (D) Noun_nom   L-Verb   (D) Noun_nom

This is the *predicate nominative* pattern, and is distinguished from pattern 5 only in its use of the noun instead of the adjective in the predicate position.

John 1:1   θεὸς ἦν ὁ λόγος   "The Word was God."
John 11:25 ἐγώ εἰμι ἡ   "I am the resurrection."
            ἀνάστασις
John 8:31   μαθηταί μού ἐστε   "You are my disciples."
John 1:14   ὁ λόγος σὰρξ   "The Word became
            ἐγένετο   flesh."

These six patterns, summarized in figure 10, are by no means the only Greek sentence patterns, but they are the most common. Because of the complexity of syntax, no one method of sentence analysis is sufficient. Theodore Mueller's *New Testament Greek* lists six basic patterns for Greek, but Mueller considers pattern 5 to be a variant of the pattern 6 kernel, listing both nouns and adjectives as "identifiers." In *The Language of the New Testament*, Goetchius considers the Greek adverb an optional constituent and so does

Figure 10   Basic Greek Sentence Patterns

With Intransitive Verbs

Pattern 1   (D) Noun_nom Verb
            τὸ πνεῦμα πνεῖ
Pattern 2   (D) Noun_nom Verb   Adverb
            καλῶς εἶπες

With Transitive Verbs

Pattern 3   (D) Noun_nom Verb   (D) Noun_acc
            ἠγάπησέν με ὁ πατήρ
Pattern 4   (D) Noun_nom Verb   (D) Noun_dat   (D) Noun_acc
            τὴν κρίσιν δέδωκεν τῷ υἱῷ

With Linking Verbs

Pattern 5   (D) Noun_nom L-Verb   Adjective_nom
            ὁ ἄνθρωπος δίκαιος
Pattern 6   (D) Noun_nom L-Verb   (D) Noun_nom
            καὶ θεὸς ἦν ὁ λόγος

not consider pattern 2 a kernel sentence. Just how many sentence patterns are really "basic" is still an open question. To expand the list in this text with some of the less common patterns would not be difficult. There are, for example, *object complement* sentences:

(D) Noun~nom~   Verb   (D) Noun~acc~   (D) Noun~acc~

In these sentences the verb takes a second accusative complement expressing an attribute of the object, as in:

John 4:46   ἐποίησεν τὸ ὕδωρ   "He made the water
              οἶνον   wine."
John 15:15   ὑμᾶς δὲ εἴρηκα   "But I have called you
              φίλους   friends."

Obviously, then, the list of kernel sentences could be expanded. But such expansion is not necessary. One can learn the essentials of any subject, including linguistics, in a practical, simplified course of study.

Expanding the Greek Sentence

How is it possible that out of the few kernel sentences listed in this section an entire language with an infinite number of sentences can be created? Two basic processes are involved, one of which has already been discussed. These will now be summarized.

One important means of generating new sentences is *suppletion*. Because the lexicon of content class words is so large, the speaker can produce an almost endless variety of combinations of nouns, verbs, adjectives, and adverbs by substituting one for another. We saw this approach at work in our discussion of the tagmeme.

But the major source of new sentence generation is *expansion*, the speaker's addition of constructions to a kernel sentence. For example, to the basic sentence Χριστὸς ἀπέθανεν ("Christ died") other information can be added to tell why, when, where, how, for whom, and so forth, he died. These expansions are not part of the basic kernel since the sentence makes sense without them. They can be viewed as a second level of syntactic relationships. Even though essential information may be transmitted through them, they are called *secondary* to indicate that they are not essential to the basic sentence pattern. Thus, in:

Χριστὸς ἀπέθανεν ὑπὲρ τῶν ἁμαρτιῶν ἡμῶν κατὰ τὰς γραφάς

the basic sentence Χριστὸς ἀπέθανεν has been expanded by means of *layering*, that is, by the addition of layers of meaning attached to the *head word*, ἀπέθανεν. Head words are generally nouns or verbs around which other words can be placed to form a *cluster*. In the above example we see how the verb ἀπέθανεν can take on two sets of attributes to form a *verb phrase*.* The words ὑπὲρ τῶν ἁμαρτιῶν ἡμῶν ("for our sins") are an expansion of the head word ἀπέθανεν indicating a beneficiary relationship, while the words κατὰ τὰς γραφάς ("according to the Scriptures") expand the verb by indicating agreement with a standard. By widening the scope of inquiry, one eventually comes to the conclusion that the entire construction is basically an expansion of the head word ἀπέθανεν. The sentence is thus reduced to a pattern 1 type, with the kernel Χριστὸς ἀπέθανεν.

Although the traditional grammarian would arrive at a similar conclusion about the kernel of the sentence, the difference between calling Χριστὸς ἀπέθανεν the subject and predicate and calling it a pattern 1 kernel is more than a difference in terminology. It is a difference in attitude. Merely picking out subjects and predicates plus a host of subordinate constructions does not account for an important fact about language—that it is composed of a series of skeletal sentences from which we form our utterances by means of expansion. Thus, equating a Greek prepositional phrase with an English equivalent is not enough for understanding an utterance. A knowledge of the syntactic relationship, that is, the specific grammatical function of the prepositional construction, is also necessary. Such relationships themselves convey meaning—structural meaning as distinguished from the meaning of words. The meaning of the total sentence consists of the interplay between these two types of meaning.

Familiarity with these syntactic relationships distinguishes the efficient Greek student. The beginning student who is not yet an efficient reader concentrates on forms but is often unfamiliar with syntactic relationships. But the knowledge of forms and of the

* Note that the term *phrase*, as used here, is not the same as that in traditional grammar. When linguists speak of a *phrase*, they mean a cluster of words structurally grouped around a head word—in the present instance, a verb. To put this another way, a phrase is any construction consisting of a head word (noun or verb) that often has attributes clustering around it to give additional layers of meaning.

meanings of prepositions is of little value without an understanding of the various functions which they possess.

What we have said thus far is purely introductory. It is now
necessary to show how the immediate environment of the head
word can be expanded into the noun phrase and the verb phrase
using the slot-and-filler approach.

Expanding the Noun Phrase

Turning to the specific means of expanding the noun phrase, let
us begin by taking the noun ἀνήρ ("man") as a nucleus and try to
fill in the slots around it. The most obvious expansion that comes
to mind is the article: ὁ ἀνήρ ("*the* man"). Unlike English, Greek
has only one type of article, namely, the definite article (Eng. *the*).
However, the absence of the article in Greek is itself of significance. In actuality, the speaker has made a decision to select what
can be called a *zero article*, symbolized by ∅, which carries with it a
kind of meaning of its own. In Greek, the presence of the article
indicates *specific identity*, whereas the absence of the article indicates
quality (characteristics).

The article is an important signal for identifying an upcoming
noun phrase. However, there are other forms that can take the
place of, or be used with, the article. We can say οὗτος ὁ ἀνήρ
("*this* man"), ἐκεῖνος ὁ ἀνήρ ("*that* man"), τις ἀνήρ ("*a certain* man"),
πᾶς ὁ ἀνήρ ("*all* the man"), or αὐτὸς ὁ ἀνήρ ("the man *himself*").
All of these forms—articles, demonstrative pronouns, indefinite
pronouns, and so forth—come under the general heading of
determiners, and all are included in this class because they may be
used interchangeably, but cannot be used in combination (except
with the article). Each determiner agrees with its noun in gender,
number, and case. Further, there are additional choices available
when the optional plural form is used with the noun head: οὗτοι,
ἐκεῖνοι, τινες, πάντες, and so forth. Moreover, this is the one noun
phrase category that must be filled; all others, save for the nuclear
noun itself, are optional.

The next way of expanding that comes to mind is by adding an
adjective: ὁ ἀγαθὸς ἀνήρ ("the *good* man"). This type of expander is
called a *modifier*. Notice that it is possible to add a long string of
modifiers to a noun phrase, as in Romans 12:2:

τὸ θέλημα τοῦ θεοῦ, τὸ ἀγαθὸν καὶ εὐάρεστον καὶ τέλειον
"The good and acceptable and perfect will of God"

Because we can add as many adjectives as we like, we can say that this is one slot in the noun phrase that is *recursive*. Furthermore, the adjective, like the determiner, agrees with its noun in gender, number, and case. This system of agreement between the various elements of the noun phrase insures that each phrase is clearly identified. Notice especially that in a noun phrase with an article, the adjective occurs between the article and the noun, as in the example above, or else after the noun with the article repeated before the adjective (ὁ ἀνὴρ ὁ ἀγαθός). Awareness of this pattern insures avoiding confusion between the noun phrase and the basic pattern of a linking verb plus an adjective in the predicate nominative relationship (sentence pattern 5).

Our sample noun phrase is further expanded by filling the *attribute* slot, which involves those devices that specify some attribute of the noun. This category is much less definite, but it too can be filled by several types of fillers: the noun, used attributively; the adverb, normally a temporal adverb, or an adverb of place; the noun phrase, filled by a phrase in the genitive case, or by a prepositional phrase; and the clause, filled by a relative clause, a participial clause, or an infinitive clause. Thus we can expand our phrase to read:

ὁ Πέτρος ὁ ἐν τῷ πλοίῳ ἀγαθὸς ἀνὴρ τοῦ θεοῦ ὃν εἶδον
θέλοντα λαλεῖν τῷ Ἰησοῦ
"Peter, the good man of God in the boat, whom I saw wanting to speak to Jesus"

To understand the slot-and-filler analysis of the noun phrase, you might refer to figure 11, which illustrates the complexity of the noun phrase with examples from the New Testament. The

Figure 11   Specimen Noun Phrases

1. Παῦλος δοῦλος Χριστοῦ Ἰησοῦ κλητὸς ἀπόστολος ἀφωρισμένος εἰς εὐαγγέλιον θεοῦ
   "Paul, a servant of Christ Jesus, called an apostle, separated unto the gospel of God"
2. πάτηρ ἡμῶν ὁ ἐν τοῖς οὐρανοῖς
   "Our Father who is in heaven"
3. σὺν Μαριὰμ τῇ ἐμνηστευμένῃ αὐτῷ οὔσῃ ἐγκύῳ
   "with Mary, who was engaged to him, being pregnant"
4. εἰς τὴν βασιλείαν τοῦ υἱοῦ τῆς ἀγάπης αὐτοῦ
   "into the kingdom of his beloved Son"
5. τὴν ζωὴν τὴν αἰώνιον ἥτις ἦν πρὸς τὸν πατέρα
   "eternal life which was with the Father"

figure shows the flexible nature of Greek word order in the noun phrase. Close study will also reveal the function of each of the slots, which in tagmemic analysis is considered to be more important than their identification.

Our discussion of syntax thus far has dealt with nouns or noun phrases expanded through a variety of means. However, in the following examples from the New Testament, other structures have assumed the syntactic role normally taken by a noun:

An adjective:	μακάριοι οἱ καθαροί
	"Blessed are *the pure*" (Matt. 5:8)
An adverb:	τὰ ἄνω φρονεῖτε
	"Set your mind *on things above*" (Col. 3:2)
A prepositional phrase:	τὰ περὶ Ἰησοῦ τοῦ Ναζαρηνοῦ
	"*The things* concerning Jesus of Nazareth" (Luke 24:19)
A particle:	οἱ μὲν ἔλεγον
	"*Some* were saying" (John 7:12)
A participial clause:	ὁ πιστεύων εἰς αὐτόν
	"*The one who believes* in him" (John 3:18)
An infinitive clause:	τὸ ζῆν Χριστός
	"*To live* is Christ" (Phil. 1:21)

These examples demonstrate the need for using more than one criterion for grammatical description. This point is important. No word out of context can be absolutely identified as a certain part of speech. Despite the fact that ἐκεῖ generally occurs as an adverb, in καὶ λέγει τοῖς ἐκεῖ—"And she says to them who are there" (Matt. 26:71)—it is syntactically a noun. Furthermore, once a given word has been employed as a particular part of speech, it can be used predictably in the same manner again.

Expanding the Verb Phrase

As we have seen, the normal active sentence contains a verb or verb phrase as one of its principal constituents. A verb phrase consists of a verb and all the words and word groups that belong with the verb and cluster around it. In many languages, such as Spanish and Greek, the verb is the central constituent, the obligatory part of the sentence. For example:

> Spanish: *Voy.*   "I am going."
> Greek: βαίνω.   "I am going."

In these examples, the subject is marked in the verb itself, so that an independent noun or noun phrase is unnecessary. The verb itself is the head word, while the other words and word groups modify and complement the verb.

Verb modifiers are of two general types. The one-word modifiers are the adverbs, which we studied in sentence pattern 2. We can classify the most common kinds of adverbs as expressing time, place, and manner.

The remaining modifiers are various kinds of word groups operating to modify the verb head word. They are the following:

Prepositional phrases

Most Greek prepositions possess a *locative* meaning, though many other ideas can be expressed by means of a prepositional phrase. The preposition is said to *govern* a case, that is, it requires that the noun that depends on it be used in the specified case— genitive, dative, or accusative. The prepositional phrase has no fixed position in the sentence. The most common functions of prepositional phrases are the following:

Place:	Μαριὰμ ἐν τῷ οἴκῳ ἐκαθέζετο "Mary was sitting *in the house*" (John 11:20)
Time:	πρὸς καιρὸν πιστεύουσιν "*For a while* they believed" (Luke 8:13)
Direction:	ἤγαγεν αὐτὸν πρὸς τὸν Ἰησοῦν "He brought him *to Jesus*" (John 1:42)
Purpose:	ἐγράφη δὲ πρὸς νουθεσίαν ἡμῶν "It was written *for our instruction*" (1 Cor. 10:11)
Beneficiary:	ἐγὼ περὶ αὐτῶν ἐρωτῶ "I am asking *on their behalf*" (John 17:9)
Reference:	γνώσεται περὶ τῆς διδαχῆς "He will know *concerning the teaching*" (John 7:17)
Instrument:	δικαιώσει περιτομὴν ἐκ πίστεως "He will justify the circumcision *by faith*" (Rom. 3:30)
Intermediary:	εἰρήνην ἔχομεν διὰ τοῦ κυρίου ἡμῶν Ἰησοῦ Χριστοῦ "We have peace *through our Lord Jesus Christ*" (Rom. 5:1)

Cause: ἐν τούτῳ πιστεύομεν
                 "For this reason we believe" (John 16:30)

Source: ὑμεῖς ἐκ τοῦ Θεοῦ ἐστε
                 "You are *from God"* (1 John 4:4)

Manner: ἠρνήσατο μετὰ ὅρκου
                 "He denied it *with an oath"* (Matt. 26:72)

Association: ὁ λόγος ἦν πρὸς τὸν Θεόν
                 "The Word was *with God"* (John 1:1)

Substitution: εἰς ὑπὲρ πάντων ἀπέθανεν
                 "One died *in place of all"* (2 Cor. 5:14)

Noun phrases

Noun phrases without a preposition are used in the verb cluster to modify the verb head or the head with other words, as in:

ἦλθον ἡμέρας ὁδόν
"They traveled *a day's journey"* (Luke 2:44)

οὗτος ἦλθεν πρὸς αὐτὸν νυκτός
"He came to him *during the night"* (John 3:2)

ἐντυγχάνει τῷ θεῷ
"He prays *to God"* (Rom. 11:2)

ἀπεθάνομεν τῇ ἁμαρτίᾳ
"We have died *with respect to sin"* (Rom. 6:2)

ἀνεῖλεν Ἰάκωβον μαχαίρῃ
"He killed James *with the sword"* (Acts 12:2)

πέπαυται ἁμαρτίας
"He has ceased *from sin"* (1 Peter 4:1)

ἐγὼ χάριτι μετέχω
"I eat *with thanks"* (1 Cor. 10:30)

Subordinate verb clauses

Subordinate verb clauses are those word groups that have a subject and predicate and begin with words like *before, since, because, unless, when, in order that,* and so forth. These words are sometimes called *subordinating conjunctions.* Unlike relative pronouns, they have no function within the clauses they introduce. They state a relationship such as cause, time, or condition, and constitute the clause part of a larger grammatical construction, as in:

καὶ ὅτε ἐγένετο ἡ ὥρα, ἀνέπεσεν
"*And when the time came,* he sat down" (Luke 22:14)

ἡ κρίσις ἡ ἐμὴ δικαία ἐστίν, ὅτι οὐ ζητῶ τὸ θέλημα τὸ ἐμόν
"My judgment is righteous, *because I do not seek my own will*" (John 5:30)

Participial clauses

A participle with its complement may be used to modify the action of the head verb. The tense of the participial construction expresses *relative* time rather than *absolute* time: the present tense usually indicates that the action of the participle occurs *concurrently* with that of the head verb; an aorist or perfect participle usually denotes an action *preceding* that of the head verb; a future participle generally indicates an action *following* that of the head verb. However, tense must be inferred from the context, and often a variety of interpretations are possible. Likewise, the significance of the participial clause is determined by its relation to the head verb and the context. Note the following:

πιστόν με ἡγήσατο θέμενος εἰς διακονίαν
"He considered me faithful *by placing me in the ministry*" (1 Tim. 1:12)

καὶ ἐβαπτίζοντο ἐξομολογούμενοι τὰς ἁμαρτίας αὐτῶν
"And they were being baptized *because they were confessing their sins*" (Matt. 3:6)

πῶς ἡμεῖς ἐκφευξόμεθα τηλικαύτης ἀμελήσαντες
"How shall we escape *if we neglect so great a salvation?*" (Heb. 2:3)

Infinitive clauses

A verb in the infinitive may also be used to modify the verb head word. The subject of the infinitive, if expressed, is in the accusative, so that the reader must decide from the context whether an accusative is a subject or a verb object. The infinitive clause may stand by itself or be introduced by either the genitive article or by a preposition plus the article in the case required by the preposition. Examples are:

πρὸ τοῦ σε Φίλιππον φωνῆσαι εἶδόν σε
"*Before Philip called you* I saw you" (John 1:48)

καὶ ἀνέστη ἀναγνῶναι
"And he stood up *to read*" (Luke 4:16)

ἤλθομεν προσκυνῆσαι αὐτῷ
"We have come *to worship him*" (Matt. 2:2)

μετὰ τὸ ἐγερθῆναί με προάξω ὑμᾶς
"*After I have risen* I will go before you" (Matt. 26:32)

To summarize, then, we have pointed out some of the ways in which the relationship of words and other units of discourse can be treated from a structuralist point of view. We have left unmentioned many other important aspects that are significant in the exegesis of the New Testament. What is clear is that the teaching of Greek syntax is going through a major transition. But regardless of whether structural linguistics is offered as a school subject, the need remains for a language student to be familiar with the linguist's approach to sentence structure.

Transformations

This is perhaps the logical point for a brief description of transformational-generative grammar (TG). Up to this point we have been studying Greek grammar from a structuralist point of view. Now we will observe another kind of grammar that is quite different in its aims and procedures.

The basis of TG grammar was outlined in chapter 1. There we saw that this grammar proposes to generate (not merely describe) an utterance from the moment of its vague conception in the speaker's mind, down to its finite, specific grammatical form—in other words, from its deep structure to its surface structure. The transformationalist begins by generating a limited number of basic sentences or kernels that are somewhat equivalent to those of the structuralist. All sentences that are not kernel sentences are defined as *transformations*, that is, variations, expansions, extensions, or permutations of kernel sentences. The major task of the transformationalist is to state the rules by which kernels generate all the possible sentences of a language. By means of certain rigorous procedures, the surface structure of the kernel sentence is rearranged in strict accordance with the rules; but the alteration is only on the surface. The deep structure remains unaffected by the surface rearrangement.

The easiest way to understand transformations is by studying them directly, and the best one for introductory purposes is the rule that explains how an active sentence can be transformed into a passive one. *Passive voice* is the structural state in which the action of the verb is directed at the subject of the sentence. Whereas the traditional grammarian felt intuitively that there was a connection between active and passive sentences, the transformational grammarian tries to make explicit the basis of this intuition by stating the rules underlying this connection.

Given a sentence like ὁ κύριος λύει τὸν δοῦλον, the first stage of transformational analysis consists of breaking the structure down into its immediate constituents and expressing this relationship by means of *phrase structure rules*, or *rewrite rules*. The first rewrite rule is:

$$S \rightarrow NP + VP$$

where *S* stands for *sentence*, and *NP* and *VP* stand for *noun phrase* and *verb phrase*, respectively. The symbol → means "is rewritten." Plainly stated, this rule indicates that the basic underlying concept of the sentence may be rewritten as a noun phrase plus a verb phrase. This does not mean that every sentence in its final form actually consists of a noun phrase and a verb phrase, in that order. What this basic statement does say is that underlying every sentence in its final form is the concept *NP + VP*, altered and shaped by succeeding procedural statements and transformations. Some of you may be tempted to reread this statement as "S → Subject + Predicate," which is acceptable, provided that you realize that you are making a statement about the *function* of the elements in this procedure, and not the *structure* itself.

With this in mind we observe that the *NP* in our sample sentence is ὁ κύριος and the *VP* is λύει τὸν δοῦλον. These two parts are the main constituents of the sentence. However, if we wanted to analyze this sentence further, we could take the *VP* and divide it as we did before, using this rule:

$$VP \rightarrow V \, (=verb) + NP$$
$$\qquad\quad λύει \qquad\qquad τὸν \, δοῦλον$$

The two groups of words left unanalyzed in the sample sentence (ὁ κύριος and τὸν δοῦλον) are both noun phrases with identical structure. We can describe these phrases as follows:

Figure 12   Tree Diagram

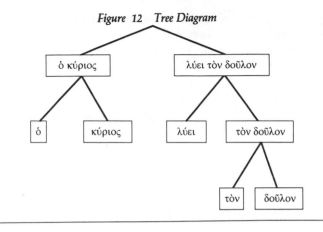

NP → D (=determiner) + N (=noun)
       ὁ, τόν   κύριος, δοῦλον

At this point we have provided a set of rules that describes not only this sentence but also many others of similar structure. These same rules could, for example, apply to ἡ γυνὴ ἀγαπᾷ τὸν κύριον, and ὁ μαθητὴς βλέπει τὸν κύριον. And, by adding just a few more rules to this set, we could describe many of the most common sentences in the Greek language.

The layers of the constituents that make up a sentence may also be represented on a *tree diagram*—so called because its parts resemble the branches of a tree (see fig. 12). In a tree diagram, a basic sentence type branches downwards in ever increasing complexity.

In addition, each node on the tree can be labeled, so that the whole construction becomes clearer (see fig. 13). The first *NP* consists of the determiner ὁ and the noun κύριος; the *VP* consists of the verb λύει and the *NP* τὸν δοῦλον which, in turn, consists of the determiner τόν and the noun δοῦλον.

We are now ready to see how a passive transformation can be performed on our kernel sentence. In order to arrive at the passive transformation, we must: (1) change the verb from active to passive; (2) make the object the subject by changing it from the accusative to the nominative case; and (3) make the subject the object of the preposition ὑπό, which requires that ὁ κύριος be put into the genitive case. Letting X represent ὁ κύριος and Y represent τὸν δοῦλον, the concise statement of this passive transformation, the *T-passive rule*, would read as follows:

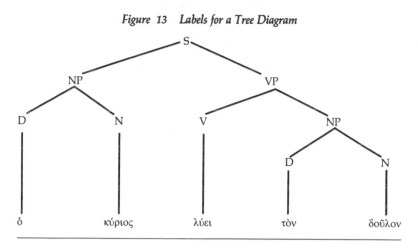

Figure 13 Labels for a Tree Diagram

$$X_{nom} + V_{act} + Y_{acc} \Longrightarrow Y_{nom} + V_{pass} + ὑπό + X_{gen}$$

The double arrow means "transformed into." Of course, the order of these elements in Greek is not fixed as it is in English, *except* that the preposition ὑπό must always immediately precede the element X_{gen}. After performing the T-passive rule on our kernel sentence, we would have:

ὁ δοῦλος λύεται ὑπὸ τοῦ κυρίου.

In similar fashion we could transform the kernel into

a *negative* sentence:	ὁ κύριος οὐ λύει τὸν δοῦλον.
an *imperative* sentence:	λύε τὸν δοῦλον.
an *embedded* sentence:	οἶδα ὅτι ὁ κύριος λύει τὸν δοῦλον.

and so forth.

TG grammar becomes much too complex, from this point on, to be treated adequately in a book with limited scope. It is hoped that the reader at least sees the similarities and contrasts between structural and transformational grammars. It should be evident, for example, that the tree diagram and other transformational devices permit a much closer scrutiny of the language than any other system devised thus far. But TG is a growing, changing system. Already linguists on the forefront of knowledge are developing new systems and expanding present ones, including TG. This merely proves the obvious: since language is changing constantly, no system of grammar will ever become the final and ultimate one.

Throughout this discussion of Greek syntax, we have focused upon the orderly forces at work in the arrangement of surface elements to achieve structural meaning. These should show us that mankind's most universal commodity is not a haphazard affair, but a consistent system capable of virtually limitless possibilities.

But I want to end on a cautionary note. You should not delude yourself into thinking that you now have learned all there is to know about the syntactical workings of New Testament Greek. This would be a false comfort. At present there is a great interest among biblical scholars in various linguistic theories, and *stratificational grammar*, developed by Sydney Lamb and his colleagues at Yale University, is increasingly recognized as an important development in the science of language. Moreover, some aspects of syntax that we have mentioned in this chapter have been included not because they were more important than others but because they are too commonly neglected or inadequately understood. Once again, nothing in language is a closed issue. New concepts are constantly being advanced, discussed, debated, praised, and sometimes condemned. Nonetheless, we should be encouraged, rather than dismayed, by this fact. My hope is that this overview will be the starting point for your *own* work with Greek syntax and your continuing, developing interest in all aspects of language.

Suggestions for Further Reading

In addition to the sections on syntax in the grammars by Funk and LaSor (see bibliography to chapter 2), good discussions of Greek syntax can be found in the following:

Greenlee, J. Harold. "The Importance of Syntax for the Proper Understanding of the Sacred Text of the New Testament." *Evangelical Quarterly* 44 (1972):131–46.

Mueller, Theodore. "Observations on Some New Testament Texts Based on Generative-Transformational Grammar." *The Bible Translator* 29 (1978):117–29.

Schmidt, Daryl D. *Hellenistic Greek Grammar and Noam Chomsky: Nominalizing Transformations.* Chico, Calif.: Scholars Press, 1981.

Case grammar theory is presented in Theodore Mueller's *New Testament Greek: A Case Grammar Approach* (Fort Wayne: Concordia Seminary Press, 1978). There are two recent college textbooks that deal primarily with structural grammar: David A. Kiefer, *New Testament Greek for Bible Students* (Lincoln, Ill.: Lincoln Christian College Press, 1975) and Donald N. Larson, *A Structural Approach to Greek, with Special Emphasis on Learning to Read the Koine Dialect* (Lincoln, Ill.: Lincoln Christian College Press, 1971). For a more traditional discussion, see James A. Brooks and Carlton L. Winbery, *Syntax of New Testament Greek* (Washington, D.C.: University Press of America, 1978).

5

Semantics: Determining Meaning

Our discussion in the previous three chapters was based on form and concerned with the analysis and description of the linguistic structure of Greek. However, meaning is what gives language its usefulness, and is its very reason for existence. It is necessary, therefore, to inquire also into the relationship between mind and expression, between the extralinguistic world of ideas and the linguistic structures used to convey those ideas.

The branch of linguistics concerned with meaning is known as *semantics*. Originally a purely historical study concerned with changes in meaning, semantics has come into its own as an important branch of biblical studies. In 1961 James Barr published *The Semantics of Biblical Language*, the fountainhead of what has come to be called the *biblical semantics movement*. In his lengthy and somewhat technical volume, Barr laid the foundation for a linguistically oriented approach to biblical lexicography. Although he was not the first to develop the basic concepts, his thorough (and sometimes undiplomatic) investigation into the area has earned a special place for him in the early development of semantic thought.

In a brief chapter such as this it is not possible to offer a comprehensive treatment of biblical semantics. A number of other writers have amplified and explained some of the principles found in *The Semantics of Biblical Language*. J. P. Louw's *Semantics of New Testament Greek* offers the most detailed introduction to the general field. Moisés Silva, in *Biblical Words and Their Meaning*, presents a fairly thorough discussion. D. A. Carson devotes about one-fourth of his *Exegetical Fallacies* to an examination of word-study fallacies. Other important works on the subject include Arthur Gibson's *Biblical Semantic Logic*, G. B. Caird's *The Language and Imagery of the Bible*, and *Lexicography and Translation*, edited by J. P. Louw. This chapter explores the terminology and methods of the biblical semantics movement, taking some basic concepts as models and looking in depth at certain areas that will serve as examples of how semantics is developed.

Etymology

The ancient Greeks debated whether the meaning of a word is to be found in its nature (φύσις) or whether meaning is a matter of convention and usage (νόμος). The Stoics opted for the former position, and through their influence the idea of ἔτυμον ("real meaning") became firmly implanted in linguistic investigation. Like the Stoics, New Testament commentators are often guilty of finding the "real meaning" of a word merely by looking up its etymology, without paying attention to the context in which that word occurs. Barr calls this the fallacy of *etymologizing*, an over-emphasis on *etymology*. However, it is a basic principle of semantics that one cannot progress from the form of a word to its meaning. Form and meaning are not directly connected, though of course the meaning of a word is usually in some fashion related to its form.

The Greek word ἐκκλησία is a notorious victim of etymologizing. Its etymology suggests the meaning, "a called-out group" (ἐκκλησία is formed from a combination of the preposition ἐκ ["out of"] and the root καλ ["to call"]). From this point on the process of etymologizing may go as far as the interpreter's imagination will allow: The church is a select group, and therefore a separatist group, called out from the rest of the world; since it is composed of people who are called, it is involved in the doctrine of election; since the calling involves a divine caller, therefore the church is an officially constituted ecclesiastical body.

In the New Testament, however, the noun ἐκκλησία does not mean a called-out group but an assembly of people defined by membership, in contrast to ὄχλος, which refers to a "crowd." In order to know what ἐκκλησία means we must therefore consider the passages in the New Testament that contain this word, not merely the word ἐκκλησία. Likewise, such statements as "sin (ἁμαρτία) means 'missing the mark,'" or "repentance (μετάνοια) means 'a change of mind'" confuse historical information with contemporary usage, and are therefore examples of etymologizing.

The proper way to use etymology and other historical information is for the sake of comparison and background, not for determining later meanings. Although a word's meaning can be related to its etymology, the relationship between the form of a word and its meaning is an arbitrary one. Hence the etymology of a word may help to determine its meaning, but only if it can be demonstrated that the speaker was aware of that etymology. Silva offers an illustration from Philippians 1:25, where Paul uses the word προκοπή to denote the spiritual progress of the Philippians. By the classical period the word had lost its original sense of "cutting down, eliminating"; it would therefore be invalid to claim that Paul is referring to obstacles that must be "cut down" before believers can go forward in their Christian lives.

Summarizing, then, the etymological method, used alone, cannot adequately account for the meaning of a word since meaning is continuously subject to change. For example, the word ἴδιος was once a strong term for "one's very own," but by New Testament times it was weakened and often occurs as a synonym for αὐτοῦ. It is therefore mandatory for the New Testament student to know whether the original meaning of a word still exists at a later stage. Above all, to know what a word means we must consider its context. Meaning is then extracted from the passage in which the word is found. Hence it is not legitimate to say that the "original" meaning of a word is its "real" meaning, unless that meaning coincides with the usage of the word under consideration.

A discussion of etymology inevitably brings up the related problem of *cognate forms*. These are a group of words in different languages that are derived from a common ancestor. The cognates of English *blood* include Swedish *blod*, Dutch *bloed*, and German *Blut*. However, few words retain their original meanings throughout their history and migration from one language to another. The English word *nice* comes from the French *niais* ("silly"), which in turn goes back to Latin *nescius* ("stupid"). The German word *Knecht* still means "servant," while its English cognate *knight* usually refers to a gentleman-soldier of high birth and privileged status. Likewise, Greek μυστήριον and ἄγων do not have the same meaning as their English counterparts *mystery* and *agony*. These examples sufficiently demonstrate that the comparison of cognates is a highly erratic and unreliable guide to meaning.

Word and Concept

It is a central concern of semantics that a clear distinction be maintained between words as linguistic units and the concepts associated with them. Although words have been used by the biblical writers to express religious meanings, concepts involve the use of far more elaborate structures than individual words. All languages have several ways of expressing a concept, and rarely does a concept consist of only one word. For example, the concept of "righteous" includes the Greek words δίκαιος, ἀγαθός, ἅγιος, καθαρός, καλός, and ὅσιος. A word study of δίκαιος alone, therefore, would hardly be sufficient as a basis for a discussion of the full and complete concept of "righteous" in the New Testament.

This confusion of word and concept, Barr complains, is one of the chief faults of Kittel's *Theological Dictionary of the New Testament* (*TDNT*). In treating individual words as if they were concepts, it implies (incorrectly) that the words themselves contain the various theological meanings assigned to them. But the meaning of words, as we have seen, is determined from the way they are used in context. These larger literary contexts, and not words, are the real linguistic carriers of theological meaning. The point is that we learn much more about the doctrine of the church from a study of the Book of Ephesians than from a word study of ἐκκλησία.

The type of word analysis found in *TDNT* unfortunately occurs also in such popular dictionaries as Nigel Turner's *Christian Words*, Léon-Dufour's *Dictionaire du Nouveau Testament*, and William Barclay's *New Testament Words*. Since these dictionaries arrange their material alphabetically according to individual words, they share *TDNT*'s methodological problem—a theological concept cannot be discussed in an article about a single word. This difficulty is alleviated somewhat in dictionaries that attempt to organize all the Hebrew or Greek words for a theological concept under an English translation of the concept (e.g., "righteous"). One such dictionary is *The New International Dictionary of New Testament Theology*, edited by Colin Brown, which is a translation and revision of the German *Theologisches Begriffslexikon zum Neuen Testament*. Better still, the United Bible Societies, under the direction of Eugene Nida, J. P. Louw, and others, is completing a major work that treats the New Testament words, not in alphabetical order, but according to some ninety *semantic domains*. The semantic-domain approach compares and contrasts all possible New Testament words for a given concept. (The theory and practice of this exciting new dictionary is explained fully in Louw's *Lexicography and Translation*.) The great advantage to this approach is that it is based upon *synchronic* (contextual) data, rather than the *diachronic* (historical) data supplied by most lexicons.

General and Secondary Meanings

Another basic assumption in semantic analysis is that words often have more than one meaning, and that within all the possible meanings of a word there is one that is used the most. Hence, each word may be viewed as having a *general* or *central meaning* and a number of *secondary* or *transferred meanings*. The general meaning of a word may be defined as the most common meaning in terms of frequency of occurrence. Linguists would also call this the *unmarked meaning* of a word, that is, the meaning that one is most likely to give when called upon to define that word. For instance, the word σπέρμα invariably brings to mind the notion of "seed" rather than that of "descendant," unless the context in which it is used requires that we take the word in a secondary or transferred sense, as in σπέρμα Ἀβραάμ ἐσμεν, "We are descendants of Abraham" (John 8:33). Likewise, the information supplied by the context will ultimately determine whether the word ἡμέρα ("day") is used in the sense of an interval between sunrise and sunset (Rev. 21:25), a twenty-four-hour period (Matt. 6:34), a time of judgment (Heb. 10:25), time in general (John 14:20), or even a court of law (1 Cor. 4:3). This last meaning is admittedly rare, yet it is the correct meaning of the word when the context is considered. Translating the word as "day" would be consistent with the general meaning of ἡμέρα but inconsistent with the context, and therefore incorrect.

The capacity of a word to have two or more different meanings is technically known as *polysemy* (Gk. πολύς, 'many' + σῆμα, 'sign, meaning'). In other words, a particular form of a word can belong to different fields of meaning, only one of which need be its semantic contribution to a single sentence or context. That is to say, there is no general or central meaning of a word that combines *all* the meanings for which the word is used. The principle of polysemy is frequently ignored in exegesis, leading to what Barr calls the fallacy of *illegitimate totality transfer*. This occurs when the various meanings of a word in different contexts are gathered together and then presumed to be present in any single context. To use Barr's own example, it would be illegitimate to presume without further indication that in any single passage the word ἐκκλησία must refer to the so-called universal church, the Body of Christ. In Acts 7:38, for example, this would clearly *not* be the meaning of the author and would actually be contradictory to the sense of the passage. Heed must therefore be given to Barr's warnings about this kind of exegesis lest in every context we bring in a word's entire semantic range. Incidentally, it is polysemy that makes a strictly literal translation such a futile exercise. This approach erroneously assumes that each word has a single meaning, and that this meaning has a precise equivalent meaning in a word of the receptor language. It is far better to determine what the potential senses of a word are, and then use all available contextual clues to select the sense that best fits the context.

Synonyms, Hyponyms, and Opposites

When different words have the same, or nearly the same, meaning, they are called *synonyms* (Gk. σύν, 'together' + ὄνομα, 'a name'). Synonymous words can be substituted for each other in given contexts with no change in meaning, as for instance, *high* and *tall*. Absolute synonyms do not exist since words always differ in some feature of meaning and, therefore, cannot be used interchangeably in all contexts. To put this in linguistic terms, synonyms do not have identical spheres of reference. We can speak of a *high mountain* or a *tall mountain*, but *he is high* means something different than *he is tall*. Nevertheless, *synonymy*, even though never complete, is an important concept in the study of meaning. It could be considered the opposite of polysemy: in synonymy two or more words may be associated with the same meaning, whereas in polysemy two or more meanings are associated with the same word.

A biblical example of synonymy involves the Greek vocabulary for "love." The relationship between the meanings of ἀγαπάω and φιλέω is such that the words may be used interchangeably in some contexts. We therefore need not be surprised that ἀγαπάω (popularly considered to refer to divine love) can describe Amnon's

Figure 14   The Hierarchy of Language

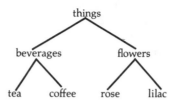

incestuous relationship with his half-sister Tamar (2 Sam. 13:15, LXX) or that φιλέω (popularly taken to refer to a lower form of love) can refer to the Father's love for the Son (John 5:20). In these contexts, both words have components of affection, desire, attachment, and so on. Other New Testament examples of synonymy are:

λόγος / ῥῆμα	"word"
ὁράω /βλέπω	"I see"
οἶδα / γινώσκω	"I know"

In each instance, the principle of *semantic neutralization* informs us that any of the terms in these pairs may be used interchangeably without any significant difference in meaning, depending upon the purpose of the biblical author.

Consideration of synonymy leads naturally to a discussion of *hyponymy* (Gk. ὑπό, 'under' + ὄνομα, 'a name'). The vocabulary of a language, at least in part, is hierarchically structured. In figure 14, general terms appear at the top of the diagram while more specific items occur at the bottom. This representation helps us see that a single generic sense includes a subset of more specific senses that share all of the generic sense's components but which are distinctive. In general, it is possible to substitute a generic sense for a specific one (such as *flower* for *rose*); but it is not possible to substitute a specific sense for a generic one (such as *rose* for *flower*) in any context when the more specific component would be inappropriate.

English vocabulary is classified this way in Roget's *Thesaurus*. Each entry has under it a list of hyponyms (words subsumed under it). The Greek lexicon of the United Bible Societies takes the same approach. It discusses, for example, the Greek terms for "ask" under the generic term αἰτέω, "I ask for." This term includes several hyponyms:

Figure 15   Componential Analysis

	bull	calf	cow
MALE	+	−	−
BOVINE	+	+	+
ADULT	+	−	+

ἀπαιτέω "I ask for something back" (Luke 6:30)
ζητέω   "I ask for something to satisfy a need" (Mark 8:11)
δέομαι "I ask for with a sense of urgency" (Luke 8:28)

Notice that each term is treated with an example of a particular occurrence illustrating the meaning in question.

Synonymy and hyponymy are valuable stylistic resources; without them a speaker would be severely limited in his ability to communicate nuances of meaning. A study of them shows that words overlap in meaning and share common properties. The word *bull*, for example, possesses the semantic properties of *male, bovine, adult*; *calf* the properties of *bovine, nonadult*; and *cow* the properties of *adult* and *bovine*. We can map out the properties possessed by each word (see fig. 15). A plus sign indicates the presence of a certain property, while a minus sign signifies its absence. This division of words and their component parts is known as *componential analysis*. Such an analysis is useful not only for nouns (as above) but also for verbs (as in the case of the Greek words for "ask").

Words of opposite meaning, like *high* and *low*, *tall* and *short*, and *happy* and *sad*, are referred to as *opposites*. The study of opposites is complex, as there are several types of opposites. For this reason, the word *antonym* is to be avoided. Some writers use it for all types of opposites, others (such as Silva) for one kind only.

The most obvious type of opposites is a pair of words in which the negative of one implies the other, as in γάμος ("married") and ἄγαμος ("unmarried"). A second type is one that is not absolute, but relative to some standard. The adjectives μέγας ("large, great") and μικρός ("small"), for example, always imply some comparison:

Matt. 28:2 σεισμὸς ἐγένετο μέγας
        "There came a great earthquake" (not a mild or
        a medium one)
1 Cor. 5:6 μικρὰ ζύμη ὅλον τὸ φύραμα ζυμοῖ
        "A little leaven leavens the whole lump" (not
        much leaven)

A third type of opposite is when one word is the *converse* of the other. The choice of one converse rather than another depends on the angle from which you view the situation being described, as in αἰτέω/λαμβάνω ("ask/receive") and δανείζω/δανείζομαι ("lend/ borrow").

Semantic Classes

In chapter 4 we saw that linguists maintain a distinction between content words and structure words, the latter being words such as prepositions and conjunctions that primarily mark syntactic relationships. However, there is in all languages another important type of distinction, that between grammatical parts of speech and the semantic nature of the terms used. The process of *semantic classification* entails recasting words so as to bring out the deep structure of their surface forms. Words may be divided into four classes: objects (things or entities), events (actions, happenings, or processes), abstracts (qualities, quantities, and degrees of the first two classes), and relationals (words showing the meaningful connections between the other three groups). These *semantic classes* may be contrasted to *grammatical classes*, which comprise the so-called parts of speech (nouns, verbs, adjectives, adverbs, and so on).

Semantic classification permits us to recognize, for example, that a number of Greek nouns are in fact semantically events (many of them derive from verbs). In Mark 1:4, for instance, the surface structure reads: "John . . . appeared . . . preaching a baptism of repentance for the forgiveness of sins" (RSV). Morphologically, there are only two verbs in this sentence, *appeared* and *preaching. John, baptism, repentance, forgiveness,* and *sins* are all nouns. Yet the only real object in the sentence is *John.* The rest of the words refer to events: John *baptizes,* people *repent,* God *forgives,* people *sin.* We can discern, under their superficial "noun-ness," their deep structure as actions. A translation made according to the deep structure is the TEV's rendering of the verse: "So John appeared in the desert, baptizing and preaching. 'Turn away from your sins and be baptized,' he told the people, 'and God will forgive your sins.'" Retaining the deep structure of the original, the surface structure has been paraphrased to bring out the essential meaning. In order to distinguish between surface and deep structures, figure 16 analyzes the Greek text of Mark 1:4. Since this verse requires so many transformations to communicate its deep struc-

Figure 16   Surface and Deep Structures

ἐγένετο Ἰωάννης . . . κηρύσσων βάπτισμα μετανοίας εἰς ἄφεσιν ἁμαρτιῶν
 | | | | | | | |
 E   O   E   E   E   R   E   E

ture, a translation such as the RSV that keeps to the surface structure is fairly difficult to understand. This illustrates the rule that the more complex the passage, the more the need to analyze it in terms of its deep structure.

One of the benefits of semantic classification is that the translator is liberated from the burden of always having to find nouns to translate nouns, verbs for verbs, and so on. He recognizes that while the semantic classes are universal, the parts of speech each language uses for surface expression are variable. Thus, the translator who works with a language where "abstract nouns" do not exist, or are stylistically awkward, is perfectly free to translate an abstract noun with another part of speech.

Ambiguity

A further aspect of meaning is the phenomenon of *ambiguity* (Lat. *ambigo,* 'I wander about'). Ambiguity in language results from the fact that there is not always a one-to-one correspondence between expressions and meanings. Here an important distinction needs to be made between ambiguity and vagueness. Ambiguity involves two or more distinct meanings for one word, phrase, or sentence, as in "I speak to you as a father" (Is the speaker or the hearer the father?). *Vagueness* has to do with lack of specificity, as in "I know some German" (How much and what sort of German?). True ambiguity (as distinguished from vagueness) is rare. When it does occur, it usually results from our ignorance of the original context rather than from the deliberate intention of the author.

Because most words are polysemous, the context is usually necessary to *disambiguate* (clarify) the meaning of the polysemous word by indicating which of the several possible meanings is intended in that particular occurrence of the word. Generally speaking, only *one* meaning of the word will be intended in any given passage. The context serves to eliminate multiple meanings. For example, no one would translate the term ὁ πρεσβύτερος in Luke 15:25 as "elder" in the technical sense because the term obviously refers to the older son in Jesus' parable of the lost son.

The meaning "elder" simply does not fit the context. Similarly, the language of John 1:9 is ambiguous apart from the larger context: "He [Christ] was the true light that enlightens every man coming into the world." The problem is whether we should take "coming into the world" with "man" or with "light" (both are grammatically possible in Greek). But the larger context, with its emphasis upon the incarnation of Christ (see 1:14), settles the issue: "The true light [Christ] that enlightens every man was coming into the world."

This does not mean that every instance of ambiguity in Scripture can or should be removed. Some ambiguity is obviously deliberate. The author of the Fourth Gospel is renowned for choosing ambiguous words to make an important point. An obvious example is the adverb ἄνωθεν (3:3, 7), which means both "again" and "from above." By means of this literary device, John (or better, Jesus) is able to synthesize two fundamental truths of Christianity: the believer must be *born again, from above* (supernaturally).

A similar example of ambiguity occurs in John 4:10, where the phrase ὕδωρ ζῶν ("living water") is understood by the Samaritan woman in its literal sense of "running water" in contrast with water from a cistern or a pool. This ambiguity leads, of course, to a fuller explanation by Jesus in verse 14. Again, take the Lord's statement in Acts 1:8: "You will be my witnesses" (ἔσεσθέ μου μάρτυρες). Here the genitive case of the personal pronoun μου presents us with two possibilities. Either it is the objective genitive, indicating that Jesus is the one *about whom* they would testify, or the possessive genitive, emphasizing their personal relationship with him—they are *his* witnesses. Both, of course, are true, and the ambiguity may be quite intentional.

Sometimes ambiguity is unintentional, however, and even when we take the context into consideration we are unable to resolve which meaning was intended by the author. A classic example is Philippians 1:10, where δοκιμάζειν τὰ διαφέροντα may mean either "to test the things that differ" or "to approve the things that are excellent." But such cases are striking because they are rare; and they are almost invariably due to our failure to operate in the same context as the author.

Denotation and Connotation

The spoken or written word normally conjures up a number of

associations in one's mind. Linguists, accordingly, distinguish between *denotation*, or the meaning a word has for all who hear it, and *connotation*, or the special meaning the same word may have for a limited group of speakers. Connotations may in fact be individual in their extent—that is, only one speaker may have a special connotation for a word. Each of us has some words that convey a special flavor, for us alone. The word *boar*, for example, has a very unpleasant connotation for me, thanks to a frightful childhood experience. On the other hand, because I happen to be an avid surfer, the words *wave, glassy,* and *locked-in* fill me with a much warmer glow than they would for the majority of their users. But because these individual connotations are restricted to one speaker, they have little or no communicative value.

Clearly, the question of semantics is to a large extent connected with the connotative meaning of individual words. For example, the word παιδία ("children") denotes persons who are between infancy and adulthood. Yet Jesus' use of the word in John 21:5 seems to imply that the persons concerned (his disciples) are also likely to be awkward, immature, obstinate, and impulsive. Conversely, the word τέκνα in the phrase τέκνα θεοῦ ("God's children") in John 1:12 seems to have a certain amount of positive relevance or force. It is this implied force which justifies our dealing with meanings as being connotative as well as denotative.

To summarize, connotative meaning is concerned with the emotional value attached to words. While denotative meanings are more or less fixed within a language community, connotative meanings may be highly individual, or they may apply only to particular circumstances. Some words or expressions may in fact acquire an emotive overtone for a majority of people, as for example the word κύνες ("dogs," Rev. 22:15) for "bad people," or the word ἐχιδνῶν ("vipers," Matt. 3:7) for "cunning people." Such terms have moved toward the status of taboo words, similar to four-letter words that have a constant emotive value.

Idioms

Certain combinations of words whose meaning cannot be determined from the individual meanings of their component parts are known as *idioms* (Gk. ἴδιος, 'one's own'). An idiom, in other words, represents one unit of meaning that connects to a combination of words, as in *hit the sack, put up with, run out of,* and countless others. Every language is laden with constructions peculiar to that language which cannot be literally translated into another. The Russian "How much to you of summers?" or the Spanish "How many years have you?" strike us as peculiar renderings of "How old are you?" On the other hand, a "round-trip" ticket is incomprehensible to romance-language speakers—how can a trip be "round"? All of this goes to show that semantics cannot by any stretch of the imagination be called an exact science.

Failure to recognize idioms in the New Testament can lead to unfortunate misunderstanding. In Matthew 16:17 the phrase *flesh and blood* (σὰρξ καὶ αἷμα) does not make sense if one insists on interpreting it literally. Likewise, the expression *daughter of Zion* (θυγάτηρ Σιών) in John 12:15 is used figuratively to designate "the people of Jerusalem." There are also longer idioms. The statement τί ἐμοὶ καὶ σοί in John 2:4 is not really an inquiry into what Jesus and his mother have in common, and unless an individual has learned this idiom as a whole unit he would have no way of knowing that it indicates a reaction of annoyance on the part of the speaker. Hence, if idioms are transferred literally from one language to another, they will almost certainly be misunderstood. Expressions such as "taste death" (John 8:52) and "whose mouth is full of cursing and bitterness" (Rom. 3:14) can lead to misinterpretation if they are understood in a non-figurative way.

Rhetorical Language

Discussion of idioms brings up the related matter of the consciousness and intention of the speaker. Not only do words mean many things to many people; they are also frequently charged with rhetorical connotations that sometimes say more than their lexical denotations. Thinking of meaning only in terms of lexical or syntactic items can easily lead to disregard for the crucial role of rhetorical features as signs having meaning for receptors. Fortunately, recent treatments of rhetorical criticism—such as *Style and Discourse* by Eugene Nida, J. P. Louw, and others—have helped biblical scholars recognize the significance of *rhetoric* as an important component in any theory and practice of biblical interpretation.

Rhetorical language makes several contributions to a text. The very unusualness of the language adds impact and therefore highlights and emphasizes the significance of the theme. Rhetoric also makes a text more esthetically attractive by providing a high degree of emotive impact, with the accompanying "hitting" (impact) and "drawing" (appeal). Rhetorical language may even serve to facilitate the memorization of content; this would apply especially to confessional or hymnic passages in the New Testament (see, e.g., Phil. 2:6–11; Col. 1:15–20; 1 Tim. 3:16).

The following terms used in rhetoric may appear complicated, but, like technical terms generally, are a convenience; without them we would be forced to give the definition every time we wished to refer to a device or process. The easiest way to learn the principal terms in rhetoric is to study them with an example and, where applicable, a comparison with related terms. Among the Greeks, rhetoric consisted of a storehouse of devices, the more important of which are discussed below.

Alliteration is the repetition of words beginning with the same letter, as in "the artful addition of apt alliteration." Literally, alliteration means the putting of "letter to letter" (Lat. *ad*, 'to' + *litera*, 'letter of the alphabet'). Occasionally it is extended to repetition of the same letter within a word, or to a combination of initial and medial repetition, as in "the afterlife's fanciful frolicking." Alliteration is remarkably frequent in the Book of Hebrews, especially with initial π, as in 1:1:

πολυμερῶς καὶ πολυτρόπως πάλαι . . . πατράσιν . . . προφήταις

Anacoluthon is the neuter of the Greek adjective ἀνακόλουθος, meaning "inconsequent, does not follow." The basic idea is "not following the path [κέλευθος], not keeping to the track." In grammar, the term applies to a failure to produce formal grammatical agreement. A New Testament example is Mark 7:19, where καθαρίζων agrees with nothing nearer than λέγει at the beginning of verse 18. The Book of Revelation has numerous examples, as do the writings of Paul.

Anaphora (Gk. ἀναφορά, 'a carrying back') refers to forms with the same meaning in analogous positions, as for example the word σῶμα ("body") in 1 Corinthians 12:12–26, or the phrase ἐὰν εἴπωμεν ("if we say") in 1 John 1:6–10.

Anastrophe derives from the Greek ἀναστροφή, "a turning back." It refers to words occurring in final position in a previous clause and initial position in the next clause, as in 1 Corinthians 7:27:

μὴ ζήτει λύσιν· λέλυσαι ἀπὸ γυναικός;
"Do not seek to be *loosed*. Are you *loosed* from a wife?"

Anticlimax is something "opposed to" (ἀντί) a "climax" (κλῖμαξ), the spoiling of an ending by allowing the last item to be less effective than the items preceding it, as in "He was a great man, an important man, a famous man, and an early rise." A *climax* is achieved when each stage is more forcible or dignified or impressive than the preceding one, as in the sequence "trouble . . . endurance . . . approved character . . . hope" in Romans 5:3–5. A New Testament anticlimax that puts the cart before the horse is 1 Thessalonians 1:3, "faith . . . love . . . hope"; here "hope" has the emphatic position at the end of the triad because of the eschatological thrust of the letter (though 1 Cor. 13:13 would normally require that "love" be given the emphatic position).

Antithesis (Gk. ἀντίθεσις, 'a placing in opposition') is rhetorical contrast. The words *You work, I play* represent an antithesis. A New Testament example is Romans 8:39:

οὔτε ὕψωμα οὔτε βάθος
"Neither height, nor depth."

Aposiopesis (Gk. ἀποσιώπησις, 'a becoming silent') is a deliberate failure to end a sentence under the influence of a strong emotion like anger or fear, as in "If you do this, I'll. . . ." Aposiopesis is seen in Luke 19:42:

εἰ ἔγνως ἐν τῇ ἡμέρᾳ ταύτῃ καὶ σὺ τὰ πρὸς εἰρήνην
"If only you had known today the things pertaining to peace . . . !"

Asyndeton (Gk. ἀσύνδετον, 'not bound together') occurs when a person omits one or more conjunctions that would normally link words, phrases, or sentences. A famous example is "I came, [and] I saw, [and] I conquered" (Lat. *veni, vidi, vici*). For a striking New Testament example, see the Greek of Romans 1:29–31. The opposite of asyndeton is *polysyndeton*, the superfluous repetition of a conjunction (as in the repetition of καί in Rev. 7:12).

Chiasmus is the arranging of lines crosswise, resembling the Greek letter χ (Gk. χιασμός, 'a making of the letter χ'). This inverted device is seen, for example, in John 1:1:

καὶ ὁ λόγος ἦν πρὸς τὸν θεόν, καὶ θεὸς ἦν ὁ λόγος
A B   C   C B A
"And the Word was with God, and the Word was God."

Failure to recognize chiasmus can sometimes lead to a misunderstanding of a passage (see Matt. 7:6 and Philem. 5).

Euphemism (Gk. εὐφημισμός, 'a speaking well of') is a toning-down of speech that is either too rude or harsh, as in "He passed away" for "He died." In Matthew 2:18, for example, a prophecy is quoted about Rachel crying for her children because οὐκ εἰσίν. "They are not" means, of course, "they are dead."

Hendiadys (Gk. ἕν ["one"] + διά ["through"] + δύο ["two"]) is where a single compound idea is expressed by its two parts as though they were independent, the several parts being soldered with the conjunction *and* (καί). For instance, in Luke 2:47 we read how the teachers were amazed at Jesus' "intelligent answers," not his "intelligence and answers" (τῇ συνέσει καὶ ταῖς ἀποκρίσεσιν).

Hyperbole is the use of exaggeration to emphasize, not to deceive, as in "He died a hundred deaths" or "Thanks a million!" The Greek ὑπερβάλλω refers to "an overthrowing, a shooting beyond the mark." An example is Mark 1:33: "And the entire city (ὅλη ἡ πόλις) was gathered at the door."

Irony is that rhetorical device whereby you say the opposite of what you mean, as in describing an extremely objectionable group of persons as "those charming people." Irony literally means "dissimulation," that is, a concealment of that which a thing is (Gk. εἰρωνεία). If a reader does not understand this figure, Jesus seems to be commending the Pharisees in Mark 7:9:

καλῶς ἀθετεῖτε τὴν ἐντολὴν τοῦ θεοῦ
"You have a fine way of rejecting the commandment of God."

Litotes (Gk. λιτότης, 'frugality') is the use of understatement to impress another, as in "How are you?" "Not bad." Luke is especially fond of this figure; an example is Acts 1:5: οὐ μετὰ πολλὰς . . . ἡμέρας, "after not many days."

Meiosis is Greek for "a lessening" (μείωσις) and, like litotes, is an understatement, not to be taken literally. Paul denied that he spoke "in persuasive words of wisdom" (ἐν πιθοῖς σοφίας λόγοις, 1 Cor. 2:4), though this disclaimer is obviously due to his modesty.

Metaphor (Gk. μεταφορά, 'a transference') is a picture of the literal and physical carried over to the moral and spiritual, as in John 10:11, "I am the Good Shepherd" (ἐγώ εἰμι ὁ ποιμὴν ὁ καλός). A *simile* (Lat. *similis*, 'alike') is a bit more formal, as seen in the use of ὅμοιος ("like") in many of Jesus' sayings (see Matt. 13:52).

Metonymy is the substitution of an attribute or a characteristic for the person or thing having that attribute or characteristic. If we say "Washington" and "Moscow" when we mean the leadership of the United States and Russia we are employing metonymy,

which literally means "a change of name" (Gk. μετωνυμία). In the
New Testament the occurrences of περιτομή ("circumcision," Gal.
2:9) referring to the Jews or ψυχή ("soul," Acts 2:43) meaning the
entire person are typical metonymies.

Paronomasia (Gk. παρονομασία, 'the formation of a word with a
slight change') is an intentional play on two similar words or
between two different senses of one word, as in λιμοὶ καί λοιμοί
("famines and pestilences," Luke 21:11) and φθόνου, φόνου ("envy,
murder," Rom. 1:29).

Periphrasis (Gk.) and *circumlocution* (Lat.) indicate the same thing:
roundabout speech, which is precisely the meaning of the Greek
περίφρασις and the Latin *circumlocutio*. An example is the sentence,
"There is a distinct reticence to bear arms by a majority of the
draft-age population" for "Most young men don't want to fight."
Likewise, Paul's expression *the third heaven* (τρίτου οὐρανοῦ) in
2 Corinthians 12:2 is an obvious periphrasis for "the place where
God is" or "the presence of God."

Pleonasm (Gk. πλεονασμός, 'an excess') is the use of more words
than necessary, as in "He was appointed temporarily, for the time
being." Pleonasm is evident in such redundant language as
ὑμᾶς . . . ὑμᾶς in Colossians 2:13 and μᾶλλον κρεῖσσον ("more
better") in Philippians 1:23.

Zeugma (Gk. ζεῦγμα, a 'yoking together') puts together words
that do not properly go together, as in 1 Corinthians 3:2, "I gave
you milk to drink, not solid food [to eat]." This construction is
usually explained as an omission, one verb being used where two
are necessary for a full statement (ἐψώμισα, "I gave to eat," is
understood).

It is impossible to list here all the figures of speech that could be
employed in Greek, or to discuss in detail their various functions.
In the appendix to *Style and Discourse*, you will find an excellent
classification of these and other figures of speech, each accompanied
by at least one example from the Greek New Testament.

Semantic Change

As we have seen, words and phrases can have wide ranges of
meaning, depending on the context in which they occur. When a
word ceases to occur in a certain context and begins to appear in a
new one, we have *semantic change*. This does not mean, of course,
that a change in meaning must necessarily entail the disappearance

of an older usage. The word ἄρτος, for example, originally referred to "bread," but in the New Testament it also refers to anything that can be eaten, that is, "food" (see Matt. 6:11). The meaning of ἄρτος has been extended or widened, while the original meaning has also been kept, as in Matthew 12:4. On the other hand, an example of the reduction of meaning may be seen in εὐαγγέλιον, "good news," which in the New Testament developed into "*the* good news," that is, the gospel of Jesus Christ. Other examples of this process are συναγωγή ("synagogue," originally "place of meeting"), ἄγγελος ("angel," originally "messenger"), χάρισμα ("spiritual gift," originally "gift"), and διαθήκη ("divine covenant," originally "testament"). Like many technical terms, these words are automatically associated with more or less definite referents (what those words stand for).

Closely associated with expansion and restriction of meaning is the change whereby a concrete term has taken on an abstract meaning or, vice versa, an original abstraction has become concretized. An interesting example is the word ἀνάπαυσις, which originally referred to "rest." However, in Matthew 12:43 and Luke 11:24, it comes to mean "resting place," thus shifting from an abstract to a concrete meaning. Similarly, the abstract word ἔπαινος ("praise") is used in the sense of "praiseworthy deed" in Philippians 4:8.

Word borrowing as a means of vocabulary building is another interesting source of semantic change. In borrowing, two processes are possible. The borrowing language may take a word and adapt it to its own phonetic system, as in ἀββά, which is a Greek transliteration of an Aramaic word meaning "father." In this case we have a *loan word*. On the other hand, the borrowing language may literally translate into native words the separate constituents of the foreign word or expression, in which case we get a *loan translation*. Greek λαμβάνειν πρόσωπον (lit. "to receive a face" = "to be partial") is a loan translation from a Hebrew expression with the same meaning.

The foregoing discussion emphasizes the importance of studying the history of words, that is, the development of meaning diachronically, through time. Here, as Silva points out, *TDNT* is indispensable. The aim is to follow the history of a word in its process of gradual transformation with a view to better understanding its contextual meaning in the particular document at hand.

Analyzing Discourse

The processes discussed above demonstrate that a good deal of what gets communicated through language is "unspoken" in the sense that it involves conveying meanings other than or in addition to the literal meaning of what is said. The importance of this fact emerges clearly in the analysis of *discourse*—any structural segment of language that is longer than a single sentence. Just as we are seldom interested in isolated morphemes, so we are rarely concerned with words as separate entities. A spoken or written word in isolation may have many different possible meanings, but a discourse, which is the environment in which words exist, imposes limitations on the choice of possible meanings and tends to shape and define the meaning of each word. In fact, language users rely so heavily on the broader discourse that almost invariably the ongoing coherence of any verbal exchange or any utterance longer than a sentence cannot be understood without it.

Unfortunately discourse analysis is one of the least understood branches of biblical linguistics at present—this despite the publication of J. P. Louw's *Semantics of New Testament Greek*. Unlike most traditional approaches to Greek grammar, this work considers the paragraph as the basic unit of semantic analysis. Word and sentence analyses are not discarded, but their significance is restricted by their participation in the broader discourse. This implies a radical departure from the "word-bound" methods of most New Testament Greek lexicons.

Following Barr, Louw stresses the importance of the word, not as a unit in itself, but as part of a larger totality, the speech in which the word occurs. It is the new setting of words, rather than the words themselves, which forms the vital contribution to New Testament thought. The distinctiveness of the Bible is therefore not to be found at the lexical or morphological level, but at the syntactic level. Hence the entire text must be taken into account before the meanings of its component words and sentences can be determined. This means that the same sequence of words can have a different meaning in a different context. For example, the well-known words ἐν ἀρχῇ ἦν ὁ λόγος, in an appropriate context, could mean "the treasurer was in the midst of a body of troops."

Since the paragraph is the largest unit of language possessing a single semantic message, Louw considers it to be the most important for the interpretation of a text. However, because paragraphs are generally too large to handle from the outset, the most convenient starting point for the analysis of a discourse is what Louw refers to as the *colon* (Gk. κῶλον), the most tightly structured syntactical unit. Roughly speaking, a colon consists of a *nominal element* (or subject) and a *verbal element* (or predicate), both of which may be expanded by elements which are dependent upon the head words. In its shortest form a colon may consist of a single word in which the subject is included as a verbal suffix, as in δίδωμι, "I give." Such a combination of subject and predicate is the major characteristic of languages worldwide. Other colons may be considerably more complex in their structures, displaying a considerable number of additions linked either directly or indirectly to either of their two basic elements.

The many examples given by Louw present some of the more complex aspects of discourse analysis, yet the most important semantic principle that they illustrate is that every separate word receives "real" meaning only within the whole text. For Louw, words do not have any meaning, but different *usages*. *Sentences* have meaning. And what is true of the relation of individual words in a sentence is true of the relation of individual sentences in a whole discourse. In the final analysis, the meaning of the smaller unit is always determined by its broader context. This means that the entire text is instrumental, if not decisive, in choosing between the different possible meanings of words and sentences.

The study of semantics is currently one of the most exciting and rapidly developing fields in linguistics. Much progress is being made, not only in New Testament Greek, but in the semantics of other languages as well. The benefits of recent studies in semantics for the Bible student are many, and only a sample can be mentioned here.

In the first place, semantics gives the exegete a framework for biblical interpretation. It ought to go without saying that everyone engaged in interpreting the Scriptures must have a set of principles, methods, and procedures for explaining as accurately as possible the meaning of the text. The more knowledge of semantics the interpreter has, the more intelligently and critically he can catch the full import of the Bible for himself, rather than determining meaning on the basis of a head count of commentators.

Semantics also provides the exegete with insights based upon a science that focuses on the nature of language and linguistic systems in general rather than on one or a few languages. For example, through the principles of componential analysis, linguistics can provide a rational and demonstrable basis for the understanding of the crucial components that constitute the meanings of key terms. The application of componential techniques could, for instance, specify which meanings of βαπτίζω are necessary and fundamental, and which are accessory, or account for the relations of meaning of prayer terms such as εὐχή, προσευχή, δέησις, and ἔντευξις.

Finally, semantics provides techniques that enable the exegete to identify both what is and what is not linguistically implicit in the original text. The use of transformations, for example, permits us to change the overt grammatical structure of an expression in a variety of ways without materially altering the meaning. Thus, for instance, the same facts are conveyed by τῆς σωτηρίας ὑμῶν and σώζει ὑμᾶς; grammatically σωτηρία is a noun, yet in its deep structure it belongs to the domain of events. In other words, transformations permit us to arrive at a formulation that says the same thing in a different form with minimal loss or distortion.

In emphasizing the contributions that semantics can make to exegesis, it should be stressed again that semantics is not a panacea and certainly not the single discipline necessary for valid interpretation. Several scholars, most notably Jacob van Bruggen in The Future of the Bible (1978), have raised legitimate concerns about the wholesale application of transformational concepts to the biblical text. If Paul decided to write "our salvation" instead of "he [God] saves us," should we not respect the form the author chose for this text? Can, in fact, the new methodology provide an objective means for determining the deep structure of a text, so that we can tell when "the love of God" is a transformation of "God loves us" and when of "we love God"? Or, again, are we to rely on mere intuition to decide whether a word is an object, an event, an abstract, or a relational?

These questions merely illustrate the fact that linguists must still arrive at a really satisfactory definition of "meaning." They must still give a more accurate accounting for the way in which the sound sequences of any language are paired with their meanings. Moreover, if extralinguistic information (which includes gestures and intonation) is an indispensable feature of the semantic component, as the evidence seems to indicate, then biblical linguists must determine how this is to be incorporated in the standard grammars of Hebrew and Greek. The work of accomplishing all these goals should provide absorbing material for study in the years ahead.

Suggestions for Further Reading

The following is a list, by no means exhaustive, of studies devoted in part or in whole to the semantic theories presented in this chapter. Each selection will require close, careful reading.

Barr, James. *The Semantics of Biblical Language.* London: Oxford University Press, 1961.

Black, D. A. "Hebrews 1:1–4: A Study in Discourse Analysis." *Westminster Theological Journal* 49 (1987):175–94.

Boyer, James L. "Semantics in Biblical Interpretation." *Grace Journal* 3 (1962):25–34.

Carson, D. A. *Exegetical Fallacies.* Grand Rapids: Baker, 1984.

Erickson, Richard J. *James Barr and the Beginnings of Biblical Semantics.* Notre Dame, Ind.: Foundations, 1984.

Hill, David. *Greek Words and Hebrew Meanings: Studies in the Semantics of Soteriological Terms.* Cambridge: Cambridge University Press, 1967.

Longacre, Robert. "Some Implications of Deep and Surface Structure Analysis of Translation." *Notes on Translation* 45 (1972):2–10.

Louw, J. P. "Discourse Analysis and the Greek New Testament." *The Bible Translator* 24 (1973):101–18.

_____. *Semantics of New Testament Greek.* Philadelphia: Fortress, 1982.

Louw, J. P., ed. *Lexicography and Translation.* Cape Town, South Africa: Bible Society of South Africa, 1985.

Mitchell, Christopher. "The Use of Lexicons and Word Studies in Exegesis." *Concordia Journal* 11 (1986):128–33.

Nida, Eugene A. *Componential Analysis of Meaning: An Introduction to Semantic Structures.* The Hague: Mouton, 1975.

Nida, E. A., J. P. Louw, A. H. Snyman, and J. V. W. Cronje. *Style and Discourse, with Special Reference to the Text of the Greek New Testament.* Cape Town, South Africa: Bible Society of South Africa, 1983.

Silva, Moisés. *Biblical Words and Their Meaning: An Introduction to Lexical Semantics.* Grand Rapids: Zondervan, 1983.

Thiselton, A. C. "Semantics and New Testament Interpretation." In *New Testament Interpretation: Essays on Principles and Methods,* ed. I. Howard Marshall. Exeter: Paternoster, 1977.

Ullmann, Stephen. *The Principles of Semantics.* Glasgow: Jackson, 1959.

Vines, J., and D. Allen. "Hermeneutics, Exegesis, and Proclamation." *Criswell Theological Review* 1 (1987):309–34.

Vorster, W. S. "Concerning Semantics, Grammatical Analysis, and Bible Translation." *Neotestamentica* 8 (1974):21–41.

Werner, John R. "Discourse Analysis of the Greek New Testament." In *The New Testament Student and His Field*, ed. J. H. Skilton and C. A. Ladley. Phillipsburg, N.J.: Presbyterian and Reformed, 1982.

6

Historical and Comparative Linguistics: The Biography of Greek

Language, like sand dunes in the desert, is a constantly changing phenomenon. It is important, therefore, for the student of Greek to be aware of the change that has taken place in the three thousand-year existence of the Greek language. Once he discovers that the character of the language has changed during this period of time, that the changes are by and large consistent, and that the whole of this change is entirely natural, he should at least be more tolerant of those variations and innovations that crept into Koine Greek subsequent to the classical period.

Thanks to the rigorous methodology worked out by nineteenth-century scholars, it is apparent that a number of diverse languages were at one time a single language and that differences came about through subsequent divergence. It would seem quite appropriate, therefore, that we should devote the final chapter of this book to a discussion of historical and comparative linguistics, that branch of linguistics which attempts to trace the histories of languages and to set up correspondences between related languages. After a brief overview of the family of languages to which Greek belongs, we will continue our historical survey of the language in chronological order, moving from prehistoric times to the modern period. Our survey will also include a brief look at the most significant features of the koine period, and at the relationship of English to Greek. We cannot pretend to cover adequately the history of the Greek language in the space of a single chapter. The field is vast, and the laborers have been many. However, it will suffice if from this overview you can understand in general terms something of the development of Greek—its origins and the kinds of changes it has undergone in its long and illustrious history.

The Indo-European Family of Languages

Greek belongs to the *Indo-European* family of languages. There are other families: the Semitic (which includes biblical Hebrew), the Ural-Altaic, and the Sino-Tibetan, for example. The term *family* means that at some time and in some place a community of people developed, over many years, a language that each generation passed on to the next. When the community outgrew its living space, part of it moved on. Then there were two groups which no longer had contact with each other. Eventually linguistic changes affecting each group became so great that intercommunication was no longer possible. This splitting process could be repeated until there were many different descendants of the parent language.

The ancestral form of the language family that includes Greek is called *Proto-Indo-European*. We do not know what the people who spoke this form called their language, since they left no records. They probably lived in southeastern Europe more than five thousand years ago. Eventually groups of Proto-Indo-European speakers broke off from the main community in repeated migrations, gradually spreading throughout Europe and western Asia from India to Britain. Separated from one another, they developed mutually unintelligible varieties of the original tongue. Greek, Latin, Sanskrit, and Russian are varieties of Indo-European, as are English, French, and German. Although these languages may be related, the changes that took place in them are quite different.

Although various European languages were compared in the Renaissance, it was not until the end of the eighteenth century that systematic comparative linguistic study began. The stimulus for this study was provided by European interest in Sanskrit, the ancient language of India. Sanskrit writings were studied and compared with other languages; consequently the relationship of Sanskrit to both Greek and Latin could not be denied. Many cognates were obvious: the form meaning "father" was πατήρ in Greek, *pater* in Latin, and *pitar-* in Sanskrit; "is" had the form ἐστί in Greek, *est* in Latin, and *asti* in Sanskrit; "three" appeared as τρεῖς in Greek, *tres* in Latin, and *trayas* in Sanskrit. Lists of similar cognates were easy to compile. It was soon evident that Sanskrit and Greek had come from a common ancestral language. Migrants using this language must have penetrated northern India at some time in the distant past and remained as a linguistic group, eventually acquiring a writing system and leaving records of a language older than Homeric Greek.

The study of other languages using comparative linguistic methodology proceeded with zeal, and it was eventually determined that most of the languages of Europe and some in Asia were related and necessarily derived from a common source. Continued study determined that the Indo-European family was divided into a number of branches, of which the principal ones are the following:

1. Indian	4. Greek	7. Balto-Slavic
2. Iranian	5. Albanian	8. Celtic
3. Armenian	6. Italic	9. Germanic

A brief discussion of the principal branches of Indo-European is useful in showing that Greek is only one of a number of languages, scattered over a wide area, that have developed in the course of time from a single source. It is also pertinent to see that, if Greek was of surpassing importance to the world in the first century A.D., its importance was not because of its linguistic superiority or the remarkable virtue of its speakers, but was due to a long series of historical events.

Indian

Indo-European speakers penetrated northern India from the west, moving into the region of the Indus as early as 2000 B.C. They acquired a writing system in about the eighth century B.C. and produced important religious literature called Vedic Sanskrit, the language of the sacred Vedas. The Vedic records are of inestimable value to linguists, since they preserve the earliest known forms of the Indo-European language. Indian Indo-European flourishes today in dialects called Prakrits, as distinguished from earlier forms of Sanskrit.

Iranian

Iranian is spoken in Iran, formerly Persia. Similarities between Iranian and Sanskrit suggest that Indo-European speakers, moving eastward, occupied the Iranian plain before a group of them moved farther east into the valley of the Indus. The earliest form of Iranian can be divided into an eastern language, called Avestan, and a western language, called Old Persian, the language of Cyrus the Great and his successors Darius and Xerxes. Persian became the dominant language and survives today, with an admixture of foreign words. There is an extensive literature in Middle and Modern Persian which was brought to the attention of English speakers by Fitzgerald's translation of *The Rubaiyat* of Omar Khayyam.

Armenian

The Armenian branch of Indo-European has been spoken in the Caucasus Mountains of southern Russia since prehistoric times. Isolation in rugged mountain country has helped Armenian communities retain their ancestral tongue, but improved schooling may yet lead their descendants to forego Armenian in favor of the dominant language on either side of the Turko-Russian border. There is a considerable literature in the language, but it has not attracted much international notice.

Greek

Indo-European speakers moved into the area of the Aegean around 2000 B.C., acquired a writing system in about the eighth century B.C., and formed a brilliant society during its classical period (the fifth and fourth centuries B.C.). A great body of literature survives as its memorial, a literature that is still read in its original language. In the classical period Greek separated into a number of dialects: Doric in the west, Ionic in the east, and Aeolic in the north. A variety of Ionic called Attic, which was spoken in Athens, became the dominant dialect to which other Greek speakers eventually conformed. This dialect became a lingua franca in the eastern Mediterranean during the time of the Macedonian Empire, and remained so for a long time after, which accounts for its use in the New Testament. Greek was the language of the Byzantine Empire until the latter's destruction by the Turks in the fifteenth century. For nearly four hundred years thereafter, the Greek language was culturally submerged. When Greece became an independent nation, Greek speakers had the problem of refurbishing their language with a vocabulary suited to the modern world, a vocabulary they preferred to derive mainly from the classical past. This refurbished Greek was a partly artificial language not readily intelligible to speakers of the vernacular. The relative propriety of the two kinds of Greek is still a matter of sometimes heated debate among Greeks.

Albanian

Albanian is spoken in a small area northwest of Greece on the eastern Adriatic shore. The territory has been dominated at various times by Greeks, Romans, Turks, and Slavs, and the Albanian vocabulary has been enlarged accordingly. There is a limited literature in Albanian, but it has attracted less attention than the literature of other Indo-European languages.

Italic

Italic Indo-European takes its name from the Italian peninsula, where Indo-European displaced other languages spoken in the peninsula, including Etruscan. In the course of time Italic split up into a number of dialects, of which Latin was one. When Rome came to dominate Italy, so did Latin. The expansion of the Roman Empire planted Latin in Iberia, in Gaul, and in the Balkan area. Latin survives today in many forms over large areas of the world: as Portuguese and Spanish in the Iberian peninsula and in Central and South America; as French in France and Canada and as a cultural language in those countries of the Near East, Asia, and Africa that were part of the French Empire; as Italian, the Latin that stayed home; and as Romanian. In addition to these major descendants of Latin, there are several minor forms: Catalan is spoken in northeastern Spain; Romansch is a minority language in Switzerland; and Walloon, spoken in Belgium, is a variety of French, as are Cajun in Louisiana and Canadian French in Quebec. The spread of Latin and its survival are matters of great historical and linguistic interest. Because surviving examples of the written language are more than two thousand years old, the study of linguistic change in Latin is richly rewarding.

Balto-Slavic

This branch of Indo-European is divided into Baltic and Slavonic. Baltic has two living forms: Lettish (the language of Latvia) and Lithuanian. A third variety, Prussian, perished in the seventeenth century when its speakers came to prefer the dominant language of Germany. A similar fate may overtake Lettish and Lithuanian, since these are now minority languages dominated by Russian.

The other sub-branch, Slavonic, is much larger. It has East, West, and South divisions. East Slavonic is subdivided into Great Russian, the official language of Russia, and Little Russian, the language of millions of speakers in the Ukraine. West Slavonic is represented by Polish, Czecho-Slovak, and Sorbian. Polish is spoken by perhaps as many as forty million speakers. Czech and Slovak are similar enough to be compounded; Czech is spoken in the western part of Czechoslovakia, with the capital, Prague, as its focal point, while Slovak is spoken in the largely agricultural eastern part of the country. Sorbian exists as a linguistic island in a German sea in the vicinity of Dresden, and can be expected to eventually disappear. South Slavonic consists of Bulgarian, Serbo-Croat, and Slovenian. Bulgarian was the first slavonic language to be recorded, largely because of Christian missionary efforts in the ninth century. Serb, Croat, and Slovenian are spoken in Yugo-slavia, with Serb having the largest number of speakers.

Celtic

Celtic Indo-European was once spoken in western Europe from Germany to Gibralter and Ireland, but has been retreating before Italic and Germanic for two thousand years and may perish completely in the near future. Caesar's conquest of Gaul doomed Gaulish Celtic, as its speakers came to adopt Latin. Celtic has a dwindling number of speakers in Britain, Ireland, and Brittany occurring in two principal dialectal varieties, called Britannic and Gaelic. Britannic Celtic has two surviving forms: Welsh, the language of Wales, and Breton, a dialect of Brittany in northern France. Political autonomy, a dream of some militants in both areas, seems unlikely, and both Welsh and Breton seem doomed.

Gaelic, the other branch of Celtic, has three living dialects: Irish, Scots, and Manx. Manx is spoken on the Isle of Man, in the Irish Channel, and is drifting toward extinction. Scots Gaelic also appears to be fading, as improved communications make the Highlands more readily accessible to English speakers. Gaelic survives in Ireland, though not all the citizens of Ireland know much Gaelic and not all of them by any means are in sympathy with the idea of a Gaelic "revival."

Germanic

By the time of the historian Tacitus (ca. A.D. 90), Germanic speakers were numerous east of the Rhine, in the Baltic islands, and in Scandinavia. But linguistic evidence makes it clear that Germanic had been a distinct branch of Indo-European for centuries before the beginning of the Christian era. By the fifth century A.D. Germanic speakers spilled over the Rhine into Gaul, Iberia, Africa, and Italy, eventually establishing new nations out of the wreckage of Rome. Some of them, called Angles, Saxons, and Jutes, crossed the English Channel and relocated in Britain.

Linguists divide Germanic into three varieties in the early historic era, called East, North, and West. East Germanic was Gothic, spoken for a time in the area of the Black Sea. Gothic does not survive, though a form of it was spoken as late as the sixteenth century in the Crimea. North Germanic is the name given to four Scandinavian languages: Swedish and Danish, forming an eastern subdivision, and Norwegian and Icelandic, comprising a western subgroup. West Germanic has two subdivisions, High and Low, these being topographical terms. High West German covers the mountain area of southern Germany, Switzerland, and Austria, and since the seventeenth century has been the literary language of northern Germany as well. Low West German in the early historic era had four distinguishable varieties. Old Low Franconian, which survives today as Dutch and Afrikaans, was a variety of Dutch spoken in South Africa. Old Saxon was spoken by those Saxons who did not migrate to Britain, and survives in the various dialects of Plattdeutsch in northern Germany. Old Frisian was spoken in the Frisian Islands of Holland and Germany, and is still spoken today by a minority. Finally, Old English was common to migrant Angles, Saxons, and Jutes in Britain. Passing through many changes since these speakers began leaving records of their language, English survives as a significant international language in today's world.

The Story of Greek

Having briefly outlined the Indo-European language family, let us go back to the prehistoric time when our linguistic ancestors wandered about central Europe, grazing their flocks and unwittingly spreading their language to the far corners of the earth. We shall confine our historical study to Greek partly because it is of greatest interest to us, and also because it has been studied so extensively. From the early speculations of Sir William Jones on the similarities of Sanskrit and Greek, linguists have been tracing, analyzing, and studying the heritage of both languages, and Greek has received a considerable amount of attention. The result is that we have a surprisingly good account of what the Greek language is and how it got that way.

Looking at the Greek language as a whole, it is possible for us to distinguish five periods in its history, dated approximately as follows:

Early Greek	2000–900 B.C.
Classical Greek	900–330
Koine Greek	330–A.D. 330
Byzantine Greek	330–1453
Modern Greek	1453–Present

These divisions, although useful as a way of presenting information, must be considered only as convenient notations. People did not wake up on New Year's Day, 1453, and begin speaking Modern Greek. The dates merely indicate the approximate time when there had been sufficient and significant change from the general character of the language at the height of the preceding period. In addition, the designations of the periods are from *our* point of view. Throughout history, speakers of Greek have always automatically considered themselves to be speaking Modern Greek. At any point in the history of Greek the language adequately served the needs of its speakers.

Early Greek

The speakers of Proto-Indo-European probably settled north of the Black Sea and the Caucasus Mountains around 3000 B.C. By about 2000 B.C. their division into separate groups had already occurred, and their first migrations into the southern part of the Balkan Peninsula may have begun. The people of this migration referred to themselves as *Hellenes* (οἱ Ἕλληνες), to their country as *Hellas* (ἡ Ἑλλάς), and to their language as the *Hellenic language* (ἡ Ἑλληνικὴ γλῶσσα). We call them *Greeks* (Lat. *Graeci*), the name given to them by the Romans, who applied to the entire people a name properly restricted to the Γραῖοι, a Hellenic tribe that took part in the colonization of Italy.

Up to 300 B.C. there were three distinct groups of Greek speakers: the Ionians, the Aeolians, and the Dorians. The Ionians were the first to migrate to Greece, but most of them were pushed out of the peninsula by successive waves of migrants. Many of them moved eastward across the Aegean to find a home on the shores of Asia Minor. Because the Asian nations knew the Ionians before they knew any other Greeks, they used the term *Ionians* as the general name for the Greeks. In Hebrew the Greeks were called the *benē Yāwān*, "the sons of Yawan," a name which is identical with Ion, the mythical ancestor of the Ionians. One group of Ionians remained on the Greek mainland, where they settled in Attica, the district around Athens. At a later time not only the Ionians but the other Greeks as well founded colonies in Libya, Cyprus, Crete, Sicily, southern Italy, Marseilles, and around the coast of the Black Sea, including the Crimea.

Classical Greek

The classical period, also called the *age of the dialects*, extends from 900 B.C. to 330 B.C., from the time of Homer to Alexander's conquest of the oriental world. In this period the dialects became localized in the districts which they were to continue to occupy throughout their existence. Conditions were in striking contrast to those in Italy, where the unification under Rome embraced the linguistic as well as the political sphere, so that Latin, at first confined to one tiny community, ultimately became the official language of the entire peninsula. In contrast to this, so long as Greece remained independent, her various regional dialects were also independent, and no single dialect became standard or official. Because of the importance of Athens in both politics and literature, its dialect was destined to become especially prominent. But the proclivity of many modern grammars to treat Attic Greek as "the most cultivated and refined form of the Greek language" (Goodwin, *A Greek Grammar*, p. 4), and divergences from it in other dialects as abnormalities, is linguistically indefensible. Classical Attic is merely a dialectal variation of the *one* Greek language and is in no sense to be regarded as the standard form of Greek, any more than we are to make Koine Greek the norm.

The classical period is said to begin with Homer because the *Iliad* and the *Odyssey*, poems about the Trojan War attributed to him, are the earliest examples of Greek literature. Homeric Greek is fundamentally Old Ionic, with an admixture of Aeolic. With some modifications, Hesiod (ca. 800 B.C.) used the language of Homer. Prose was written by the Ionians in the sixth century, and Ionic was used in the fifth century by Herodotus (484–425) and Hippocrates (b. 460). As Athens gained cultural as well as political prominence, however, the Attic dialect became the language not only of dramatic dialogue, but also of literature in general. In it were written the tragedies of Aeschylus, Sophocles, and Euripedes, the comedies of Aristophanes, the histories of Thucydides and Xenophon, the orations of Demosthenes, and the philosophical works of Plato and Aristotle. Generally speaking, Classical Greek is Attic Greek in terms of extant Greek literature.

With the Macedonian conquest Athens ceased to produce great writers, but the Attic culture and dialect were diffused far and wide. With the extension of its range, Attic Greek, slightly modified by the languages with which it came into contact, became the κοινὴ διάλεκτος, or "common dialect" of the world.

Koine Greek

The period of the κοινή may be dated roughly from the death of Alexander the Great around 330 B.C. to the building of Byzantium by Constantine in A.D. 330. This "common" dialect was the language of the New Testament, and its use facilitated the spread of Christianity. Attic Greek, by virtue of its prominence (Alexander himself had spoken Attic), provided its basis, but as the new lingua franca it absorbed several non-Attic elements and underwent a degree of grammatical simplification. The term *Hellenistic Greek* is sometimes given to that form of the Koine which was used by the Jews of Alexandria who produced the Septuagint and by the writers of the New Testament, all of whom were Hellenists, foreigners who spoke Greek (Gk. ἑλληνίζω, 'I speak Greek'). But no accurate distinction can be made between the terms *koine* and *Hellenistic*.

Alexander's conquests in Asia and Africa had established Greek for many centuries as the common language of the lands bordering the eastern Mediterranean, including the Holy Land. When Palestine was incorporated into the Roman Empire in 63 B.C., Greek continued to be spoken along with Latin, the official language of the empire. In the city of Rome itself Greek was used as much as Latin, so that when Paul wrote his letter to the Roman Christians he wrote it in Greek. Indeed, throughout the first and second centuries A.D. Greek appears to have been the chief language of the Roman church, although Latin was making headway and soon superseded it.

The historians Polybius, Diodorus, Plutarch, Cassius Dio, and Josephus, the rhetoricians Dionysius and Lucian, and the geographer Strabo used the Koine. Several writers of the koine period sought to reproduce the "purity" of the earlier Attic. These *Atticists* flourished chiefly in the second century A.D. Lucian (A.D. 120-180) is perhaps the best example. However, it is generally agreed that the New Testament has more in common with the nonliterary Koine than with the artificial and archaic style of the Atticists.

Byzantine Greek

The term *Byzantine Greek* is applied to the form of Greek current from the time of Constantine to the fall of Byzantium to the Turks in A.D. 1453. Byzantine Greek is, generally speaking, a continuation of the Koine. During this period scholarship nearly ceased in Greece proper, and it was in Byzantium and Asia Minor that scholarly studies in Greek were kept alive. By far the largest group of Greek New Testament manuscripts are those copied during the Byzantine era.

Toward the end of the twelfth century the popular Greek then spoken in the Byzantine Empire began to appear in literature beside ancient Greek, which had ceased to be intelligible to the common people. This popular language, the earliest form of Modern Greek, was called *Romaic* ('Ρωμαϊκή) because its speakers chose to call themselves *Romans* ('Ρωμαῖοι), the capital of the Roman Empire having been transferred to Byzantium (Constantinople). The contrast between an idiom based on ancient models and one more in agreement with popular speech gave rise to a conflict lasting into modern times.

Modern Greek

Modern Greek, which can be dated from the fall of the eastern Roman Empire, is the language spoken by about ten million people inhabiting two states, Greece and Cyprus. It constitutes the present stage in the natural development of the language from the ancient Hellenes to the modern Athenians.

Greek speakers today must learn two fairly distinct sets of linguistic patterns. The official language, called the Katharevousa (Gk. καθαρεύουσα, the "purifying" language), is standard for virtually all written communication and is spoken only for official purposes (in the Greek Orthodox Church, the Greek parliament, and so on). The spoken language, called the Demotic (Gk. δεμοτική, the "people's" language), is the normal language for oral communication and is written only in less formal literary contexts. The gap between the written and the spoken language is greater than in any other European language, and attempts to bring the literary language nearer to the spoken have met with little success.

Modern Greek is written with the same alphabet as ancient Greek, and the main body of vocabulary has been handed down from classical times with its spelling virtually unchanged. Naturally the pronunciation has altered in the course of time; a lapse of two millennia is bound to produce changes in any living language. The letter β, for example, is no longer pronounced as b, so that βίβλος today sounds like *vivlos*. However, the pronunciation of Modern Greek is basically the same for both varieties of the language, as far as this is not modified by modern Greek dialects (found especially in Cyprus, Crete, and northern Greece).

As prescribed in the textbooks used in the schools, Modern Greek retains three case forms of the adjective, noun, and article, along with the three gender classes. It has dropped two tense forms (perfect and future) that are replaced by analytical constructions. In ancient Greek, for example, a form like "I shall loose" was expressed simply by λύσω; today the particle θά (a contraction of θέλω) is put in front of the present form (θά λύω) or the indefinite form (θά λύσω), meaning "I shall be loosing" and "I shall loose," respectively. Otherwise, Modern Greek has not moved very far from the elaborate inflectional system of Classical Greek. The official language of Modern Greece, as written though not as pronounced, would undoubtedly have been intelligible to Plato.

Today, the influence of Greek extends far beyond the shores of the Aegean. Beginning in the sixteenth century Greek words, disguised by Latin, came into English usage. In the nineteenth century a steady trickle became a torrent. Each of us uses every day, possibly without knowing it, many words in "international Greek"—*telephone, gyroscope, hippopotamus, perimeter,* and hundreds of others. Of course, our forefathers might well have been content with *far-sounder, spiral-viewer, river-horse,* and *around-measure.* They might have been, but they were not. Whether for snobbish or practical reasons—and there were probably both—new inventions, new fields of study, new combinations of ideas were given names made of Greek components. "At no other time in our history have there been so many words of Greek origin on the lips of the English-speaking peoples," writes Frederick Bodmer in *The Loom of Language* (p. 246). Greek, as a quarry for word building, is by no means "dead" in English.

Modern Greek as well as Classical Greek has an important contribution to make to the study of Koine. The Demotic does not differ materially from the vernacular Byzantine, and thus connects directly with the vernacular Koine. The intermediate position of New Testament Greek (between Classical and Modern Greek) is obvious not only in grammar but also in pronunciation and vocabulary. Tendencies seen in Koine syntax have become normative in the Modern Greek vernacular (e.g., the disappearance of the optative and the infinitive). The pronunciation of Modern Greek is often seen in the manuscripts of the New Testament and other Greek documents. Sometimes, too, the Modern Greek lexicon can illumine New Testament vocabulary. For example, the word παρασκευή (John 19:14, 31, 42) is the Modern Greek word for "Friday." This fact supports the interpretation that the expression *the preparation (παρασκευή) of the passover* means "Friday in passover week," rather than "the day before passover."

The learning of Modern Greek is experiencing a revolution and no Greek student can afford to ignore what is happening. The School of Modern Greek of the University of Thessaloniki has pioneered the teaching of Modern Greek to foreigners and the preparation of materials for such teaching. Fourteen teachers from the university have cooperated in the preparation of *Modern Greek for Foreigners* (1981), while three of the fourteen have produced *The Language of Idioms and Expressions* (1983). *Modern Greek for Foreigners* is graded for beginning, intermediate, and advanced levels, and also contains a supplement on the Katharevousa. The student of the New Testament has much to learn about the Koine idiom in the light of Modern Greek, and the main features of Modern Greek outlined in these books offer an excellent introduction to the present-day language.

Such in brief is the history of this fascinating language that forms such an important part of our own, a history of change and yet of amazing perseverance. Greek is an admirable instrument of communication, eminently fitted to serve as the tool of the rigorous thinker and of the inspired prophet alike. We who cannot hear ancient Greek cannot hope to fully appreciate it. Pitch alone must have given a musical quality even to ordinary speech. Poetry was actually sung, and in prose, too, attention was paid to rhythm and euphony. The New Testament was meant to be heard rather than seen; ancient reading was reading aloud, and even the simplest passage must have expressed delicate nuances of grammar and diction.

But we need not think that Greek was or is the most perfect expression of human thought in the world. Both English and Greek are rich languages, but their richness lies in different areas. Whereas Greek has an abundance of verb endings, English prefers to use analytical expressions. Greek and English are simply languages at different stages of development, English having moved from complexity of form to simplicity. We therefore need not rhapsodize about the wealth of Greek forms ("The development of tense has reached its highest in Greek, and presents its greatest wealth of meaning" [Dana and Mantey, 177]). Judged in the only way a language can be judged—as a means of communication— neither Greek nor English nor any other language will be found wanting.

Major Characteristics of Koine Greek

To say that the New Testament was written in Koine Greek does not mean much unless we understand what is meant by that designation. At this point in our historical survey of the language, let us therefore endeavor to characterize the most important features of the Koine.

The word *koine* is simply an English transliteration of the feminine form of the Greek adjective κοινός, meaning "common" (cf. Jerome's *Vulgate*, the vulgar or common version of the Latin Bible). When applied to the Greek language, the word has a threefold significance: historically, it refers to the language spoken during a certain period, namely, the period extending roughly from 330 B.C. to A.D. 330; geographically, it refers to the language that was common to speakers of Greek throughout the entire Mediterranean world during that period; and culturally, it refers to the language spoken by the common people of that day, though here a further distinction can be made between semiliterary Koine, which approximated Classical Greek, and nonliterary Koine, which was used by people with little education.

Historical Development

Koine Greek represents a significant stage in the historical development of the language. Spoken and written after the "golden age" of Classical Greek had passed, it was marked by a noticeable change in pronunciation and vocabulary and by a slow but significant change in forms and constructions. Scholars studying the history of Greek are fortunate in that there exists a great deal of literature from the age of the Koine, making it possible to trace many of the changes Greek underwent during this period. The principal body of new material has been the papyri from Egypt, of which thousands have been published in the past century. They are roughly contemporary with the New Testament, and many of them are datable precisely in the first century A.D. They are unsophisticated and natural reflections of the ordinary speech of common people, and are important for the information that they give about the everyday life and language of the ancient Hellenistic world.

Three major tendencies are exhibited in Koine Greek: (1) the tendency toward semantic change; (2) the tendency toward greater simplicity; and (3) the tendency toward more explicit expression.

Semantic change

Although the Koine retained most of the word-stock of Classical Greek, it was not immune to semantic modification, nor could it have been, for it was a living language. Often certain words had simply weakened their meaning by the koine period. In Classical Greek, for example, the verb λαλέω meant "I babble" (as in child's talk), but in the New Testament it appears as the ordinary verb for "speaking," be the speaker God or man (see Eph. 4:25; Heb. 1:1–2). Likewise, the verb βάλλω, used formerly to denote a somewhat violent throwing, can mean little more than "I put" or "I send" (see Matt. 10:34; Rev. 2:24). So, too, the adjective ἴδιος is overtranslated if it is always rendered "own" as in Classical Greek; nothing is lost by saying simply "his wife" (Acts 24:24), "his father" (John 5:18), or "his farm" (Matt. 22:5).

Another feature of Koine Greek is its modification of the earlier meanings of the prepositions. A well-known example is the encroachment of εἰς (originally meaning "into") upon ἐν (originally meaning "in"), which eventually led to the complete disappearance of ἐν in Modern Greek. Attempts by earlier scholars, such as B. F. Westcott in his commentary on the Gospel of John, to discern fine distinctions between the meanings of these two prepositions in a passage such as John 1:18 ("The phrase is not strictly 'in the bosom' but 'into the bosom.' ") are clearly mistaken in the light of the papyri. Yet another example of change in meaning between the classical and koine periods is evidenced by the conjunctions. The word ἵνα, which in Classical Greek was confined to purpose clauses ("in order that . . ."), has a much wider range of meaning in New Testament Greek. When it appears in John 13:34, for example ("A new commandment I give to you, *that* you love one another"), we need not infer that brotherly love is the purpose of the new commandment, but simply that the commandment *consists in* love for one another. Again we find ἵνα used in result clauses ("so that . . ."), as when the disciples ask Jesus, "Rabbi, who sinned, this man or his parents, *so that* he was born blind?" (John 9:2). It may even be translated "when" in John 16:32: "An hour is coming, and is already here, *when* you will be scattered." So much, in fact, did ἵνα extend its range of meaning that eventually it replaced the older infinitive forms of the verb. Indeed, in Modern Greek ἵνα—shortened to νά—plus the indefinite is the regular form of the infinitive, as in γνωρίζω τί νά πεῖ, "I know what to say."

The New Testament meaning of the comparative and super-lative adjectives is also better understood when we consider their usage in Koine Greek. In the comparison of adjectives the old superlative forms were disappearing, except in the elative sense (rendered "very," as in Mark 4:1, where ὄχλος πλεῖστος means "a very large crowd" and not "the largest crowd"). On the other hand, the comparative took the place of the normal superlative, so that μείζων (the comparative of μέγας) in 1 Corinthians 13:13 can unblushingly be translated as "greatest." This tendency to use the comparative for the superlative continued until in Modern Greek the superlative idea is expressed by the use of the article with the comparative form (e.g., ὁ μικρότερος, "the smallest").

Greater simplicity

In the second place, the Koine can be said to lack the refinement of Classical Greek. This is seen, for example, in the composition of its sentences. Unlike Classical Greek, which had a wealth of connectives to express the most minute differences in the relationships of clauses, the Koine knows few conjunctions. Its favorite is καί, reflecting an unornamented style reminiscent of a small boy describing his first visit to the zoo.

In morphology, there is a general tendency toward simplification, generalization, and harmonization of inflections. The old dual verb forms have disappeared, and the μι-verbs are steadily being replaced by ω-verbs. There is a marked increase in the number of verbs ending in -ίζω, such as βαπτίζω. We find γίνομαι and γινώσκω instead of γίγνομαι and γιγνώσκω, and -τωσαν instead of -ντων in the plural of the imperative. Forms like ἤλθοσαν, γέγοναν, and εἶπαν (first aorist terminations on second aorist verbs) are common. The periphrastic tenses, especially the periphrastic imperfect, are on the rise. We also observe the leveling of middle-voice forms to active ones (as ζήσω instead of ζήσομαι) and the tendency to replace unusual or difficult forms by new ones formed by analogy (δύνασαι for δύνῃ; ἡμάρτησα for ἥμαρτον). Finally, the optative mood is disappearing. In fact, almost the only optative to survive is the optative of wishing, the most famous example of which is the Pauline formula μὴ γένοιτο, "Let it not be!"

These simplifications in Koine Greek—and many others can be noted—so greatly distinguished it from Classical Greek that several writers of the koine period launched a reactionary movement known as *Atticism*. These writers desired to make Attic Greek, as written during the golden age of Greece, the unchanging standard for pure Greek style. But these purists made the mistake of thinking that they could restore the old Attic style by imitation. Historical developments such as the rapid rise in the number of people speaking Greek and the need for a simple language for commerce made it linguistically impossible for Atticism to succeed. The short-lived revival of Attic Greek was therefore a negligible influence upon the writers of the New Testament.

More explicit expression

Koine also shows unmistakable traces of a tendency toward clarity of expression. This is characteristic of all vernaculars. In the Koine it means a preference for compound verbs over simplex forms, the use of pronouns as subjects of verbs that do not need them, the use of prepositional phrases to replace the simple cases, a preference for ἵνα and ὅτι instead of the infinitive, and the use of direct rather than indirect discourse. Adverbs pile up before and after verbs; parenthetical statements abound; redundant emphases like "the very same," "each and every," and "very great" are on the rise. There is a constant striving for clarity and explicit expression characteristic of any naive, unschooled author.

A World Speech

The Koine was "common" also in the sense that it was not divided into dialects, but rather was the vehicle of expression of all who spoke Greek in the postclassical period. There were provincial or local elements (notably in Egypt and Syria), but the Koine was not an artificial mingling of various elements but a living whole, much like a stream made up of other streams flowing into it.

The conquests of Alexander were largely responsible for creating this lingua franca. The soldiers in his army, coming as they did from all parts of Greece with its various dialects, were forced to make their speech intelligible to the whole group. It was not an artificial literary language that spread so rapidly through the world, but the vernacular of the common soldier. Thus there developed out of the numerous dialects of Greece a unified language not only for Greece but for the whole world.

The world empire created by Alexander continued to be a social and cultural unity for several centuries after his death. Along with the empire went the idea of a world-community—what the Greeks called an οἰκουμένη. There was a corresponding growth of humanitarianism and acceptance of less cultured classes of people. Hence the sharp contrast between Greek and barbarian became considerably less well defined. The Hellenization of the world had a leveling influence much like that of the modern newspaper, radio, and television. Even those who held tenaciously to their native tongues, such as the Egyptians and the Italians, knew Greek. Thus it was that the New Testament apostles could carry the message of Christ in one language and be understood wherever they went. Greek was no stranger even in the Jerusalem church, where the membership included Greek-speaking Jews as well as Aramaic-speaking Jews (see Acts 6:1).

As a whole the Koine was a single language with only minor variations—much like contemporary English in the United States or England. In other words, the Koine was homogenous, in spite of local variations. In fact, so completely did Alexander do his work that the centers of Hellenistic culture shifted from Athens to eastern cities such as Antioch and Alexandria.

A Language of the Common People

Finally, Koine Greek was "common" in that it was the language of the common people. Any lack of homogeneity in the language was due to differences of education and background and to the individual styles of those who used it. Generally speaking, the more cultured an author was, the more literary was his work. If the writer were one of the intellectuals, like Lucian, they let the Attic idiom influence almost every line they wrote. This imitation of Attic Greek hardly reflected the common language of the people, for the avowed Atticist had a style altogether different from the everyday speech of the people. But in the papyri of Egypt we have a source that truly reflects the language of the people. Although the papyri show a wide range of literary ability, they do indicate that the Koine was the language of the common people as well as the cultured in the first century A.D. Further corroboration of this conclusion is supplied by the study of the modern Demotic, which exhibits features that may be traced directly back to the vernacular of the koine period.

For the most part, the men who wrote the New Testament employed this common language of everyday life. The New Testament writers do on occasion rise to the literary heights of the Atticists, but on the whole the language of the New Testament parallels so closely the language of the papyri that there can be no doubt that it was written in the same vernacular Koine Greek. We may quote Moulton's *Grammar* for the kind of light that the vernacular papyri cast on New Testament Greek:

> The new linguistic facts now in evidence show with startling clearness that we have at last before us the language in which the apostles and evangelists wrote. The papyri exhibit in their writers a variety of literary education even wider than that observable in the NT, and we can match each sacred author with documents that in respect of Greek stand on about the same plane. The conclusion is that "Biblical" Greek, except where it is translation Greek, was simply the vernacular of daily life. Men who aspired to literary fame wrote in an artificial dialect, a would-be revival of the language of Athens in her prime, much as educated Greeks of the present day profess to do. The NT writers had little idea that they

were writing literature. The Holy Ghost spoke absolutely in the language of the people, as we might surely have expected He would.

This, then, is the language in which the New Testament was written, a language which belongs to the living stream of the historical development of Greek from the ancient Hellenes to the modern Athenians, a language which during the first Christian century was a world speech common to the entire Roman Empire, a language which was spoken by common and cultured people alike. The Koine is not simply Classical Greek on the decline, like pure gold accidentally contaminated. Instead it is like a new and serviceable alloy, powerfully blending together the various Greek dialects into a single language used by Greeks as well as non-Greeks. It is the language which, at the time when the gospel began to be proclaimed among the nations, was uniquely suited for the propagation of that message.

English and Greek

We began this chapter by discussing genetically related languages, languages that are later developments of a single earlier tongue. Both Greek and English belong to branches of a proto-language called Indo-European. Although English and Greek have long been separated from their common ancestor and have become mutually unintelligible, linguists have observed that many of the differences between the two languages can be accounted for in terms of regular phonetic changes. Quite often there will be words that have the same (or approximately the same) meaning in both languages. These words are called cognates (Lat. *cognatus*, 'related') because both have the same ancestor and neither is the result of any borrowing. For example, English *father* and Greek πατήρ are cognates since both have descended directly from Indo-European *patér* (the asterisk indicates that this word does not appear in any historical source). Because English and Greek are "sister" languages, it is possible to identify in each language many such cognates that have descended from the same primitive Indo-European word.

The attempt to relate cognates to a parent language is called *phonological reconstruction*. The initial step in this process is to group together words from languages that we suspect or know to have the same origin. Quite often we will be able to identify words with the same meanings in the attested languages, as with *father* and πατήρ. But we must also be aware of possible semantic shifts that may result in somewhat different meanings. Greek φράτηρ, for example, is a cognate of English *brother*, but its meaning is slightly different—"member of a brotherhood." (The word *brother* in Greek is, of course, ἀδελφός.)

In the initial search for cognates, it is wise to start with words that have been in a language continually for a long period of time and are not likely to be borrowings from other languages. Words such as *telephone* and *psychology* are relatively new items and generally travel from one language to another in an undisturbed phonological shape. The most useful words for reconstruction are those which represent common or universal items, such as the parts of the body, familial terms, certain natural objects like hills or trees, and so on.

It takes many sets of related forms to establish and support a historical relationship. This is because it is not difficult to find *pseudocognates* from almost any two languages. For example, in Modern Greek the word for "eye" is μάτι. The Malay word *mata* also means "eye." We see here a possible correspondence: a two-syllable word beginning with *m*, having a *t* in the middle, ending with a vowel, and sharing the same meaning. In order to establish a genetic relationship between Malay and Modern Greek, however, we would have to find many such sets, all sharing a correspondence between Greek μ and Malay *m*, Greek τ and Malay *t*, and having a Malay *a* where Greek has ι. This cannot be done, and we are safe in attributing the pair of words for "eye" to chance alone.

Through elaborate studies, linguists have determined why certain sound shifts have occurred and have even established "laws" pertaining to them. To explore these laws with profit would require a respectable background in foreign languages, ancient and modern. For our purposes, however, it is enough to know the relationship of alphabet to sound, and of sound to meaning. We need to know how these sound shifts function in order to understand which consonants are interchangeable in English and Greek.

Grimm's Law

A major discovery of the early nineteenth century was a set of sound changes that the Germanic languages underwent after their separation from the original Indo-European tongue. These changes can be formulated as rules based on such correspondences as shown in the following list:

Greek	Germanic (English)
πατήρ	father
τρεῖς	three
καρδία	heart
βύρσα	purse
δύο	two
γένος	kin
φέρω	bear
θύρα	door
χόρτος	garden

The initial phonemes in the words given above indicate consonants that correspond to each other in the two languages. The initial π in πατήρ, for example, has changed to *f* in *father*, just as the initial δ in δύο has become *t* in *two*. Since Greek is not the language from which the Germanic languages descended, the Greek forms are not the original forms from which the Germanic forms were derived. Rather, both are descended from a common source; but the consonants in Greek are closer to the original Indo-European forms and thus are to a certain extent more conservative.

Based on the above correspondences, we can summarize the Germanic consonant shift using three simple rules:

1. Where the Indo-European parent language has the voiceless stops, *p*, *t*, and *k* as reflected in Greek and Latin, the Germanic cognates (represented by English, for example) have the voiceless fricatives *f*, *th*, and *h*.
2. Where the Indo-European parent language has the voiced stops *b*, *d*, and *g* (also preserved in Greek and Latin), the Germanic cognates have the voiceless stops *p*, *t*, and *k*.
3. Where the Indo-European parent language has the aspirated voiced stops *b*^h, *d*^h, and *g*^h (preserved in Greek as φ, θ, and χ), the Germanic cognates have the unaspirated voiced stops *b*, *d*, and *g*.

These sets of changes are known collectively as *Grimm's Law*, because their systematic character was first recognized by Jacob

Figure 17   Shift Between Consonants in Greek and English

1. π, τ, κ = f, th, h.

(a) π and f.	πατήρ	"father"	father
	πολύς	"much"	full
	πούς	"foot"	foot
	πῦρ	"fire"	fire
(b) τ and th.	ὀδόντ-	"tooth"	tooth
	τρεῖς	"three"	three
(c) κ and h.	καρδία	"heart"	heart
	καρπός	"fruit"	harvest
	κολωνός	"hill"	hill
	κυν-	"dog"	hound

2. β, δ, γ = p, t, k (c)

(a) β and p.	βύρσα	"a hide"	purse
	κύβος	"loin"	hip
	τύρβη	"tumult"	thorp
(b) δ and t.	δρῦς	"oak"	tree
	δύο	"two"	two
	ὀδόντ-	"tooth"	tooth
(c) γ and k.	ἀγρός	"field"	acre
	γένος	"race"	kin
	γόνυ	"knee"	knee

3. φ, θ, χ = b, d, g.

(a) φ and b.	φέρω	"I bear"	bear
	φράτηρ	"a brotherhood"	brother
(b) θ and d.	θυγάτηρ	"daughter"	daughter
	θύρα	"door"	door
(c) χ and g.	χήν	"goose"	goose
	χόρτος	"grass"	garden

Grimm (1785-1863), one of the Brothers Grimm (who are best known in America for their collection of German fairy tales). There is some controversy over whether Grimm should be credited with discovering this law, since the list of correspondences had already been published by the Danish philologist Erasmus Rask. Grimm, however, is usually given the credit because he emphasized the lawlike properties of the correspondences.

How Grimm's Law operates can be seen in figure 17. Only words that have penetrated into Germanic after the sound shift, such as logic (Gk. λογικός), hamartiology (Gk. ἁμαρτία), and hectic (Gk. ἑκτικός), show a g = γ, t = τ, and so forth. When you use a word like paternal, you pronounce it like it was heard in primitive Indo-European; when you use fatherly, you are reflecting the operation of Grimm's Law.

Exceptions to Grimm's Law

After Grimm's Law had been accepted, various scholars began to take up the apparent exceptions and attempted to explain them by pointing out conditioning phonetic environments. One of the first of these exceptions to be explained was the case of the voiceless stops after *s*. For example, where you find τ after σ in Greek, you will find the same sound in Germanic; in other words, the environment *s-*, so to speak, prevents the operation of Grimm's Law as regards voiceless stops. Thus the Greek root στα (as in ἵστημι) remains *sta* in English *stand* (cf. Lat. *sto*, 'I stand').

In the early and mid-nineteenth century, other exceptions were also accounted for. A classic example is the law "discovered" by Hermann Grassmann (1809–1877), a noted German mathematician and Sanskritist. Certain Indo-European correspondences were causing difficulty in that they seemed to contradict previously established patterns. Grassmann examined the data in Sanskrit and Greek and was able to show that developments peculiar to these languages resulted in the apparent irregularities. For some reason the phonology of Sanskrit and Greek did not permit successive syllables to begin with aspirates. This can be illustrated by examining the Greek words τρέχω ("I run") and θρίξ ("hair") in figure 18. Notice that in each of the forms only one of the aspirated consonants occurs, but this varies in each of the two sets: in 1a and 2b we have a χ and in 1b and 2a we have a θ. In other words, in these paradigms we find aspirated consonants (θ, χ) alternating with unaspirated ones (τ, ξ) and this gives us different forms of the stem (τρεχ-, θρεξ-; θριξ, τριχ-). From the above forms Grassmann was able to deduce that in pre-Greek the original stems were *threkh-* and *thrikh-*. Greek then underwent two sound changes. The first of these removed the aspiration from the consonant when it was followed by σ; the second deaspirated a consonant when it was followed by another aspirated consonant in the same stem. By applying these rules to the pre-Greek forms we can account for what appears in the attested words. Thus in τρέχω the original aspiration in the initial phoneme has been deaspirated, though in the future it reappears. Likewise, in θρίξ the aspiration in the nominative is deaspirated in the genitive τριχός, whereas the ξ of the nominative becomes an aspirated χ in the genitive.

The significant advance here was that the phonetic environment was considered to be important, thus requiring examination of

Figure 18   *Phonological Irregularities*

1. a. τρέχω   "I run"   b. θρέξω   "I will run"
2. a. θρίξ   "hair"   b. τριχός   "of a hair"

Figure 19   *Process of Verner's Solution*

Greek	Latin	Sanskrit	Old English	
πατήρ	páter	pitár-	fáeder	"father"
μήτηρ	máter	matár-	módor	"mother"

successive syllables within a word. As it turned out, the second rule above—that two aspirated consonants may not occur in the same stem—also applied in Sanskrit and came to be known as *Grassmann's Law.*

About half a century after Grimm's Law had been laid down, the Danish scholar Karl Verner (1846–1896) was able to dispose of yet another exception by showing the importance of the position of the accent in the Indo-European languages. The problem was that in some Germanic words the consonants *b, d,* and *g* corresponded to Greek and Latin *p, t,* and *k.* From Grimm's Law, the expected Germanic correspondences should have been *f, th,* and *h.* Verner explained this irregularity by pointing out that the Indo-European *p, t,* and *k* become voiceless fricatives only when the accent in the Indo-European root word fell on the syllable immediately preceding the sound in question. Figure 19 illustrates how Verner solved this problem. From the Greek, Latin, and Sanskrit, Verner reconstructed the Indo-European ancestors **patér* and **matér.* Notice that Verner assumed the Sanskrit accent pattern was present in the reconstructed forms. By so doing, he was able to show that when *f, th,* and *h* are preceded by an unaccented vowel, they become the corresponding voiced stops. Thus, Old English *faeder* and *modor* are quite regular in their correspondence with Sanskrit *pitár-* and *matár-*. In the same way, English *hundred* (rather than *hunthred,* which would correspond to Latin *centum*) represents a regular correspondence because of the place of the accent in Sanskrit *satám.*

This exception to the Germanic sound shift, or *Verner's Law,* as it came to be called, had a crucial impact on the history of linguistics. By seeking a scientifically verifiable explanation for deviations in Grimm's Law, Verner not only justified the claim of regularity in sound changes that his "law" had purported to establish, but he was also instrumental in setting the stage for the neogrammarian school of linguistics in the late nineteenth century.

We have wandered a considerable distance from the simple introduction with which this chapter opened, but these technicalities are necessary to enable us to understand something of the circumstances in which God's revelation was recorded, so that we may better appreciate that revelation and the God who gave it. The study of the history of the language of the New Testament is an interesting and illuminating one, though it has its limitations and is not, as some would have us believe, the key to unlocking all mysteries. Nevertheless, the New Testament is an important landmark that in some cases brought about, and in other cases illustrates, a great many changes that have taken place in the long history of the Greek language.

The foregoing discussion is a reminder that the truly scientific grammar is fundamentally a grammatical history, and not a lawbook. Grammars merely record from time to time the changing phenomena of language. It is the sum total of these changes viewed in a historical perspective of scores of generations that has created a gulf between Classical Greek and the Modern Greek vernacular, though they represent one and the same language at two different stages of its history, much in the same way that an octogenarian is the same person he was at the age of twenty except for the inevitable transformations brought about by the passing of years. The study of Greek, therefore, must proceed from two points of view: the total history of the language as a branch of Indo-European, and the development of that which is unique to the New Testament. Unfortunately, the school tradition has concentrated on the latter to the almost total exclusion of the former. The impossibility of disassociating language from the sociological and historical processes from which it develops may produce new linguistic curricula that change this situation.

Suggestions for Further Reading

Definitive studies of historical and comparative linguistics include the following:

Arlotto, Anthony. *Introduction to Historical Linguistics*. Boston: Houghton & Mifflin, 1972.

Lehmann, W. P. *Historical Linguistics: An Introduction.* New York: Holt, Rinehart & Winston, 1962.

Sturtevant, E. H. *Linguistic Change.* Chicago: University of Chicago Press, 1962.

Sweet, H. *History of Language.* New York: Macmillan, 1900.

Publications of special interest to the Greek student are:

Browning, R. *Medieval and Modern Greek.* London: Hutchinson University Library, 1969.

Buck, Carl D. *Comparative Grammar of Greek and Latin.* Chicago: University of Chicago Press, 1933.

Costas, Procope S. *An Outline of the History of the Greek Language.* Chicago: Ares, 1936.

Gingrich, F. W. "The Greek New Testament as a Landmark in the Course of Semantic Change." *Journal of Biblical Literature* 73 (1954):189–96.

Mussies, G. "Greek as the Vehicle of Early Christianity." *New Testament Studies* 29 (1983):356–69.

Palmer, L. R. *The Greek Language.* Atlantic Highlands, N.J.: Humanities Press, 1980.

Postscript

Throughout this volume questions have been raised concerning relevance. By now the implications of linguistics for teachers and students of New Testament Greek should be obvious.

Among these implications, perhaps the most important is the point of view toward language that is becoming accepted because of linguistic research. Language has been demonstrated to be something that can be studied objectively like other types of human behavior. Current language research provides students with a vital body of information about language sufficient to serve both their practical needs and their need for some understanding of language as a subject in itself. For example, phonological studies that are just now coming out will likely revolutionize our teaching of Greek phonemics and spelling, so that instead of viewing the word as an arbitrary sequence of sound units without fixed patterns, we will look at it in the way presented in chapter 2—as sound features with definite patterns reflecting the application of phonological rules. Studies in the field of transformational grammar are also developing rapidly, particularly aiding our understanding of linguistic competence, that is, the way thought and expression are interrelated. It is almost certain that the distinction between deep and surface structure, discussed in chapters 4 and 5, will become an important part of the Greek curriculum, once there is more general agreement about exactly what is to be included in the deep structure.

It seems equally certain that our whole notion of lexicography will be modified by the development of more fully explicit lexicons than have been produced in the past. This development should make it easier to relate the study of words to other units of meaning such as sentences, paragraphs, and entire discourses. Unfortunately, traditional grammars still faithfully devote large amounts of space to one of the admittedly great contributions of the classical grammarians—identifying the Greek parts of speech— despite the fact that this emphasis often obscures other significant facts about the Greek sentence. No one can argue that it is useless to know that certain words are called "nouns," others "verbs," and the like. But if language study is no more than learning a set of labels, it can hardly lead to the outcomes described above.

Finally, linguistics can (and it must be admitted that this is at present more a prophecy than a fact) lead to substantive improvements in the ways in which the biblical languages are taught. The best language teaching materials are those which capitalize to the fullest extent the interrelationships between the various subsystems of language. We have seen that all the aspects of the Greek language form an integrated system; all the parts are interrelated, and their relationship seems to be hierarchical. This suggests that teaching materials should be designed so that the most widely applicable—and the most basic—concepts of descriptive linguistics are introduced from the beginning. Such materials would certainly include a discussion of the sentence, of the notion of content and structure words, and a fairly explicit definition of the terms *phoneme, morpheme, word*, and *discourse*. Good language materials will also explain the relationships between the superficially unrelated aspects of language such as grammatical analysis and historical linguistics, thus enabling students to see the whole process of communication as a kind of activity parallel to other aspects of human behavior and interrelated with all of them.

However, having examined the language descriptively, historically, and comparatively, we have not done the real job at all—we have only prepared for it. The real action lies in using the language as a medium of interpretation, of learning to function as hearers and heeders of the message God has entrusted to us (Rev. 1:3). And this involves going beyond linguistics to exegesis. It involves breaking through the myths that surround language— the myth that Greek is more advanced or more beautiful or more expressive than Hebrew or other languages; the myth that some words are superior to others merely because tradition holds them so; and finally the myth that meaning is contained in the word itself rather than in the discourse in which the word occurs.

It is to this question of meaning that students of New Testament Greek must ultimately be directed. Anything else falls short of the goal, for language without meaning is not language at all. The action is no longer with declensions or conjugations, or even with new methods of linguistic analysis. If these things justify themselves, it must be on the basis of the larger picture—of the contribution they make to the individual's ability to discover something of the infinite richness of the Greek New Testament and to make its truths more understandable to people with little or no knowledge of Greek.

The purpose of language education is therefore not to make students into apologists for (or against) a given linguistic dogma, but rather to make intelligent linguists out of them—persons who are able to think about language in other than purely subjective terms, and who have a vocabulary adequate to phrase the generalizations they come up with. Only if this book leads to a curiosity about language itself and to a sense of competence in thinking and talking about language, will it have realized the practical goals that are its ultimate justification.

Subject Index

Scripture Index